Don't Forget

To say thank you for picking up a copy of my book, I would like to provide you with four special bonuses. These are each items that will help you implement the knowledge you'll find in these pages. Remember, information without implementation is not terribly helpful!

Bonus #1: Asset Allocation Training

This training program will walk you through the process of building a customized asset allocation model. We'll talk about cash, precious metals, stocks, bonds, Bitcoin, and early stage investments… and how each fit into your portfolio.

Bonus #2: Special Report – Cornerstone of an Equity Portfolio

This report lays out the good practices around analyzing and investing in stocks. It also provides professional research and analysis on two specific stocks. These both represent a tremendous opportunity today.

Bonus #3: Training Video: How to Buy Investment Real Estate Step-by-Step

This video will walk you through the process of how to buy cash-flowing rental properties, step-by-step. With the proper resources and network, building passive income with real estate is almost as easy as buying stocks online.

Bonus #4: Full Length Course:
The Infinite Banking Concept

This course details a secret strategy for warehousing capital in a tax-advantaged way. If implemented correctly, the *Infinite Banking Concept* can build a guaranteed $1 million pension plan that will last generations.

To access your bonuses, just go here:

https://www.beyondthenestegg.com

BEYOND THE NEST EGG

How to Be Financially Independent Outside of a Broken System

JOE WITHROW

Beyond the Nest Egg

How to Be Financially Independent Outside of a Broken System

First Edition: **2023**

ISBN: 979-8-89109-106-1 - paperback
ISBN: 979-8-89109-107-8 - ebook

DEDICATION

This book is dedicated to my children, Madison Lynn and Isaiah Joseph. Please know that you two are the inspiration behind all my work. You've always been a tremendous blessing to me. I'm forever grateful for you.

And to my wife Rachel – thank you for your understanding and unwavering support. I can't tell you enough how much I appreciate it.

Calmness is the rarest quality in human life. It is the poise of a great nature, in harmony with itself and its ideals. It is the moral atmosphere of a life self-reliant and self-controlled. Calmness is singleness of purpose. It is absolute confidence and conscious power – ready to be focused in an instant to meet any crisis…

The man who is calm has his course in life clearly marked on his chart. His hand is ever on the helm. Storm, fog, night, tempest, danger, hidden reefs – he is ever prepared and ready for them.

He is made calm and serene by the realization that in these crises of his voyage he needs a clear mind and a cool head. That he has naught to do but to do each day the best he can by the light he has. That he will never flinch nor falter for a moment. And that, though he may have to tack and leave his course for a time, he will never drift. He will get back into the true channel, ever headed toward his harbor.

When he will reach it, *how* he will reach it matters not to him. He rests in calmness, knowing he has done his best. If his best seem to be overthrown or over-ruled, then he must still bow his head – in calmness. To no man is permitted to know the future of his life, the finality. God commits to man ever only new beginnings, new wisdom, and new days to use to the best of his knowledge.

Calmness comes ever from within. It is the peace and restfulness of the depths of our nature. The fury of storm and of wind agitate only the surface of the sea. They can penetrate only two or three feet. Below that is the calm, unruffled deep. To be ready for the great crises of life we must learn serenity in our daily living. Calmness is the crown of self-control.

When the worries and cares of the day fret you, and begin to wear upon you, and you chafe under the friction – be calm. Stop, rest for a moment, and let calmness and peace assert themselves…

Then, in some great hour of your life, when you stand face to face with some awful trial, when the structure of your ambition and life-work crumbles in a moment, you will be brave. You can fold your arms calmly, look out undismayed and undaunted upon the ashes of your hope, upon the wreck of what you have faithfully built, and with brave heart and unfaltering voice you may say: **"So let it be – I will build again."**

—*The Majesty of* Calmness, by William George Jordan

CONTENTS

INTRODUCTION

The world has fundamentally changed.

It used to be that a lack of information was one of our biggest challenges. Prior to the internet, finding information was much more difficult and time-consuming. It could take days, weeks, sometimes even months. Today, however, we have the opposite problem. We are inundated with incredible amounts of information all day, every day.

The problem is, most of this information is just noise. Much of it is nothing more than junk. And if we fill our heads with junk, we're far more likely to make bad decisions.

The advent of the internet and the over-availability of information is just the beginning of how our world has changed, significantly and permanently.

Like me, I suspect many can "feel" that things aren't going back to the way they used to be. At first, that's an unsettling thought. What does that mean for us? And by *us*, I mean the regular folks.

Should we keep doing things the way we always have and hope for the best? Or should we make changes? And if it's the latter, what changes should we make?

To answer this question, we must understand what's actually happening on the greater world stage. And to gain this understanding, we must cut through the smoke, the mirrors, and the biases that pervade the information we take in every day.

We must understand that there is a big difference between information—which is common—and insight—which is not. The more we can sift through the information surrounding us and focus only on the insight, the better.

And one of the best ways to do this is to learn how to cut through the fluff and analyze what really matters—incentives.

If we can get a good feel for a person or an institution's incentives, we are much better able to understand and project future actions. Then we can make our own decisions accordingly.

That is what this book is all about. It's also what prompted me to start a comprehensive investment membership that we call *The Phoenician League*. The membership strives to cut through the noise so that we can make sound financial decisions.

The Phoenician League also connects members with investment opportunities across several asset classes. These include both stocks and real estate.

The Phoenician League also helps members plug into a larger professional network. This takes all the guesswork and gruntwork out of achieving financial independence. Our goal is to help everyone work up to having $10,000 a month in extra income.

Before we can implement a strategic investment plan to make that happen, we must understand the existing financial system and what's happening on the macroeconomic stage right now.

Over the course of the next several chapters, we'll talk about exactly what's happening in the world today. We'll discuss the big economic changes that are brewing right now, and then we'll dig into the various factions that have an outsized influence on both the monetary system and the economy. We're also going to take a dive into exactly how we can structure our finances accordingly.

But first, let me give you a fair warning…

I'm going to provide you with my independent analysis. It's not going to look like anything that will ever be presented on television or in mainstream news articles. And I don't self-censor.

Those who automatically reject anything that doesn't immediately conform to their pre-existing beliefs and worldview may be a bit uncomfortable with my analysis. But if you're willing to give it a hearing, you will find that the incentives I have uncovered are hard to refute.

So, if you're willing to accompany me, let's carry on. But please buckle up. There are no paved roads where we're going…

CHAPTER ONE

A DRAMATIC BREAK ON THE GLOBAL STAGE

I spent about eight years in the world of corporate banking. That was my first career. After that, I spent nearly a decade immersed in the world of high-end–investment research. That was my second career. That's the lens through which I am writing to you today.

The focus of this book is how to get our personal finances right, in lieu of the shifting macroeconomic climate we find ourselves in. My passion is financial independence, but I don't approach this from a consumerist mindset. To me, it's all about living a purpose-driven life.

That said, there are forces at work out there that have an outsized impact on the economy and the financial system. And as I'm sure many of us have noticed, these forces have been pushing substantial changes over the last few years.

We are living through an incredible point in history. The sequence of events that take place over the next several years will shape the order of the new world.

I suspect most of us already know this to be true. We can "feel" it. We've probably felt it for several years now.

In the next few chapters, I'll summarize what I think is happening on the world stage… who the major players are… and what it means for us. There are some important actions each of us should take right now to get ahead of what's coming.

I suspect many of us realize now that the world is not as simplistic as the mainstream news presents it to be. There are power structures working behind the scenes to deliver carefully scripted narratives.

For the last several decades it certainly appeared as though those power structures were uniformly aligned. I'm speaking from an American perspective here.

Fiscal policy (Congress) worked hand-in-hand with monetary policy (the Federal Reserve). They each seemed to align with international interests.

That is to say, what happened in the US appeared to be in line with what the United Nations (UN) and the European Central Bank (ECB) wanted as well. Global policies often appeared to be coordinated. This was especially true when it came to monetary policy and interest rates.

And here's the thing—this seemed to be the case regardless of which political party happened to be in power at any given time. Political campaigns made all kinds of lofty promises, but nothing seemed to change much once the elections were over. This fueled a belief in some circles that there must be a shadowy, unified organization operating behind the scenes.

Comedian George Carlin would talk about this in his skits. "*It's a big club and you ain't in it,*" he would say.

But it has become clear that this isn't exactly true.

Instead, there are distinct factions at work. And for the first time since I've been paying attention, two prominent factions in the US appear to be at odds with each other. It took me a few years to come to this conclusion, but the evidence and the incentives are very clear.

In full transparency, my previous worldview was that the "West" consisted of the establishment, the insiders, and the rest of us.

In my previous view, the establishment was a smorgasbord of government departments, regulatory agencies, and major multinational corporations. And as I saw it, the insiders were a smaller circle of people who influenced the major policies and legislation that were pushed through.

That view could explain how big-picture policies seemed to remain the same regardless of which political party was in power. The problem is, this worldview couldn't explain the Donald Trump saga.

Trump himself was a New York insider. He ran in the Big Apple's highest circles of wealth, power, and influence.

When Trump positioned himself as a champion for the little guy in his 2016 presidential campaign, he injected the term 'Deep State' into common vernacular. Donald Trump also talked passionately about 'draining the swamp.'

This resonated with tens of millions of Americans. Donald Trump was elected president on this populist message.

At first I thought that this must be a ruse. Trump was an insider, and insiders typically don't upset the apple cart.

And sure enough, Trump did very little to drain the swamp. Sure, he cut some regulations and passed some tax reforms, but that's about it.

Trump didn't seriously challenge any federal departments or entrenched bureaucrats. He certainly didn't reduce the size, scope, and power of the federal government in any meaningful way.

Yet, what he referred to as the Deep State still hated him with a passion. And they went so far as to tamper with the 2020 election to get rid of him. They did this in plain sight for all to see by using mail-in ballots and closed-door vote counting. Some firms suggested that the voting machines were rigged to skew the votes as well.

Now, I don't want us to get caught up in the politics of it all. My point is that there was a clear effort made by elements within the power structure to prevent Donald Trump from winning the 2020 election.

Most confusing of all, they installed Joe Biden as their puppet president. Biden was a fifty-year denizen of Washington, DC. He represented the status quo perfectly. That means Biden was just an interchangeable cog in the wheel. There was nothing about him personally that stood out from any of the other DC establishment politicians.

This didn't make any sense to me.

If Trump didn't pose any serious threat to the machine, why did they hate him so much? And why did they repeatedly go after him in plain sight?

First it was the election. Then they raided his home in August 2022. Then they indicted him on thirty-four clearly exaggerated felony charges. Trump had to appear in court to answer to these false charges in April 2023.

These aggressive attacks served only to strengthen Donald Trump's political support. So why do it?

That's a question I couldn't figure out. If the mechanisms of power consisted of the Establishment and the insiders—what Trump called the Deep State—these actions simply made no sense. In my view, Trump did very little to threaten the status-quo while in office.

The events of 2022 provided us with the answer.

SOFR Explains All

In January 2022, something called the Secured Overnight Financing Rate (SOFR) went live across the board. This was the first year that SOFR became the dominant interest rate benchmark in the US.

I doubt many people have ever heard of SOFR. Of those that have, I suspect very few know what it is, or why it's so significant.

SOFR is a benchmark interest rate for dollar-denominated loans and derivatives.

We don't need to go down a deep rabbit hole on this to get the big picture. What's important to understand is that the interest rates for all loans in the US are now influenced by SOFR. That's only been the case since January 2022.

However, the Federal Reserve (the Fed) conceptualized SOFR in 2018. It appears Trump's appointed Fed Chair Jerome Powell was a key figure involved.

The appointment of John Williams as the head of the Federal Reserve Bank of New York in 2018 was also critical to this plan. We didn't realize it then, but a secret coup was in motion.

For context, the Fed consists of twelve regional banks. But the New York Fed holds the most power. That's because it houses the Open Market Trading Desk and it manages the System Open Market Account. These are the mechanisms by which the Fed conducts monetary policy.

The point is, SOFR could only come into being if it had support from the people who truly run the show at the Fed. That is to say, the Chairman and the head of the New York Fed.

To understand why this is important, we must know what SOFR just replaced.

Previously, the London Interbank Offered Rate (LIBOR) was the interest-rate benchmark for dollar-denominated loans and derivatives. That means those who could influence LIBOR could also influence interest rates in the US.

And who could heavily influence LIBOR? Among others, the Bank of England (BoE) and the European Central Bank (ECB) can have an impact on LIBOR through their own policy initiatives.

What this means is that the Fed did not have full control over US monetary policy prior to 2022. And that's what this is all about.

SOFR is based exclusively on transactions in the US Treasury repurchase (repo) market—which the Fed is directly involved in.

To summarize a complex topic, the Fed used SOFR to decouple US monetary policy from the European power structure. That was the coup.

The plan came together in 2018 under Trump's appointed Fed Chair Jerome Powell, but it didn't come fully to fruition until 2022. This is what enabled the Fed to aggressively raise interest in 2022 and into 2023, even with everybody screaming at them to stop.

If we remember, the UN came out in October 2022 and said that all central banks needed to stop raising rates. That was directed at the Fed. They were trying to reel the Fed back in, but the Fed made a decisive decision to break ranks. This was intentional.

By raising interest rates in the US, the Fed very quickly drained the Eurodollar market of liquidity. That, in turn, limited what the ECB could do with its own monetary policy. In fact, it forced the ECB and the rest of the world to follow suit and raise their own domestic interest rates.

Now, Eurodollars are simply US dollar-denominated deposits held at foreign banks, mostly European.

The Eurodollar market exists outside the US regulatory system. And it provides liquidity to European financial institutions and ultimately European governments. They can leverage Eurodollars to support spending programs that they favor.

By draining the Eurodollar market, the Fed effectively hamstrung the ECB's ability to drive its own agenda forward.

Which of course raises the obvious question: why?

As we noted earlier, the Fed seemed to be aligned with the ECB for years… maybe decades. On many occasions it appeared their policies were coordinated. The response to the 2008 financial crisis is a great example.

So why did the Fed break ranks?

Understanding this is the key to understanding why an element of the Establishment hates Trump so much. More importantly, it's critical to understanding what's playing out on the world stage right now, and how we should position our finances accordingly.

The Factions Jockeying for Power

It turns out that George Carlin's quip was too simplistic. There isn't one monolithic power structure in place calling all the shots. It's much more nuanced than that.

My own worldview was too simplistic as well. I perceived an 'Establishment' and a group of 'insiders'—but even that doesn't cover it. Instead, there are multiple factions at work.

That's certainly true here in the US. I would bet this dynamic exists in every major country as well.

To have a clearer understanding of the macroeconomic picture, we need to understand the factions competing for power.

In the US, what Trump referred to as the Deep State looks to be international in nature. This faction is driven by the old-world European powers that have been in place for centuries.

They control the UN, the ECB, and most of the other western globalist organizations. The World Economic Forum (WEF), the International Monetary Fund (IMF), the World Bank, the World Health Organization (WHO), and the Centers for Disease Control (CDC) are several great examples.

Joe Biden very clearly works for them, as does much of the national Democratic Party and some high-level members of the Republican Party.

Going forward, we'll refer to this faction as the globalist power structure.

The primary competing faction appears to be the interests behind the big New York banks. They consist primarily of J.P. Morgan, Citibank, Goldman Sachs, and Morgan Stanley.

I believe that these are the same interests who helped establish the Fed in the first place. That was back in 1913. Their power and wealth reside here in America. That's why they orchestrated a coup to liberate US monetary policy from the globalist faction.

This begs the question—why? What happened to cause the New York banking interests to break rank?

The theory that makes the most sense is as follows...

In 2020, the globalist power structure unveiled their master plan. They called it the "Great Reset."

This plan envisions a completely new way of organizing society. At its core, the Great Reset is about overthrowing whatever's left of our traditional economic system and replacing it with a grotesque version of neo-feudalism.

Of course, that's not how they positioned it.

They call their new system "stakeholder capitalism." It's supposed to sound like a friendlier version of capitalism. But there's one key question we need to ask here. *Who are the stakeholders?*

Well, it's *them*. In their vision, their globalist organizations control everything.

A big pillar of that plan is to make central banks the ultimate arbiter of everything when it comes to money and credit. That necessarily means the commercial banks need to be toned down or eliminated completely.

That's what retail central bank digital currencies (CBDCs) are all about.

With retail CBDCs, our bank accounts would reside at the central bank. This is true both for individuals and corporations. That would give the central bank full control over our money and our transactions.

Then, when we need a loan, they are the folks we would have to go to. That's huge. Especially when we consider that it's not just individuals who would have to go to them for loans. It would be everybody, including large companies. They would have to go to the globalist power structure to get financing for their business and key projects.

That means this faction would suddenly have direct control over which projects and activities could get financing and which couldn't. This alone would give these people almost total control over the western world.

Again, this plan requires the commercial banks to be neutered or eliminated. That's the key.

And that's why the Fed and the New York banks broke rank. We'll explore this dynamic in more detail in the next chapter.

Key Points

I'll include this "Key Points" section at the end of most chapters. This section will be brief, but it will make everything we've discussed actionable for you.

This section will start by simply highlighting the key points and takeaways from the chapter. I'll also include supporting external resources where I can. They will help you digest the material in this book.

Here's our summary for Chapter One:

- We are living through an inflection point in history
- The world is not as simplistic as the news makes it out to be
- For the last several decades the existing power structures have been pulling in the same direction… but that recently changed
- Today, the two prominent factions in the US are the European-aligned globalists and the New York banking interests—and they are at odds with each other
- The Fed pulled off a silent coup by replacing LIBOR with SOFR
- The Fed's rate-hiking campaign wasn't about fighting inflation—it was about draining the Eurodollar market
- The globalists want a "Great Reset"—that's what the CBDC push is all about

CHAPTER TWO

CONTROL OVER THE ENGINE OF FINANCE

To help solidify our understanding of this complex subject, we need to talk at a high level about the banking system as it's currently constructed.

What we have today is called a "fractional reserve" banking system. The name stems from the fact that commercial banks can issue more loans than they have reserves for. More specifically, the fractional reserve banking system allows the commercial banks to issue loans at a 10-to-1 ratio relative to reserves.

As the Austrian School economists point out, this effectively gives commercial banks the ability to create money from nothing—just like the central banks can do. Bob Murphy de-mystified the system succinctly in his book *Understanding Money Mechanics.*[1]

Let's illustrate this concept with a simple example.

---

1 https://mises.org/library/understanding-money-mechanics-0

Suppose I go out and borrow $10,000 from my local bank. Where does that money come from?

Many people believe the bank lends out the money accrued via its deposits, but that's not at all what happens. In fact, if this were true, the bank would need to take $10,000 out of somebody else's account and lend it to me, the borrower. They don't do that.

Instead, the bank simply credits my account with $10,000 when they issue me the loan. This is money that did not exist before. And it is money that will disappear again when I pay the loan back.

The thing is, the bank must back my loan by at least 10 percent in reserves. In this example that means it must have at least $1,000 on deposit that's not already serving as reserves for somebody else's loan.

What's important to understand here is that the fractional reserve system allows the commercial banks to finance a lot more projects than it could if it had to maintain a one-to-one reserve ratio.

This allows the banks to determine what gets financed and what doesn't. As you might imagine, there's an immense amount of power in this, especially when we start talking about projects that are foundational to society.

For example, should we finance new oil and gas projects and small-module nuclear reactors… or acres upon acres of windmills and solar farms?

Should we finance small local farms… or should we push all agriculture into a few multinational corporations?

Should we provide seed financing to promising small businesses… or only support larger corporations?

The ability to aggregate and allocate capital is absolutely critical to modern civilization. Those who control the engines of finance have an outsized ability to shape our world.

And here's the thing—there's fierce competition among the commercial banks. This ensures that each bank strives to make good credit decisions. The better their loans perform, the more money, power, and influence they accumulate. So, they want to finance the most promising companies and projects.

This is why our standard of living has risen so dramatically over the last 120 years. The banks have financed new energy technology… new agriculture methods… and all kinds of other projects that have helped us reduce scarcity.

As a result, even people of below-average means in the developed world live a life that's far more comfortable than the richest people alive just over a century ago.

Now, I need to pause here and acknowledge that the fractional reserve banking system isn't the hero of this story. It has plenty of flaws that disadvantage those of lesser means.

However, the fact that the commercial banks utilize the current system in a highly competitive way is what's important. There are very strong incentives for the banks to only finance those projects that are economical. And to be economical, those projects typically need to benefit a large number of people.

Coming full circle here, the globalist power structure wants to usurp this power. That's what their Great Reset is about. They want to monopolize the banking function so they decide which projects get funding and which don't.

And—importantly—they want to eliminate all competition so that there are no direct consequences for financing uneconomical projects. This would allow them to favor pet projects specifically designed to restructure society according to their aims.

That's what the CBDC push is really about.

Yes, CBDCs would make it easy for the globalist power structure to track and monitor all our transactions. With this, they would be able to freeze our transactions if they didn't like what we were doing. I know there are a lot of people out there pushing back against this power grab. I certainly support this push-back.

But the thing is, this isn't an entirely new dynamic.

Our bank and credit card transactions are an open book. If somebody with the right influence really wanted to, they could freeze our bank accounts today—no CBDC necessary.

Sure, a CBDC would make this easier on them. And we should absolutely oppose it accordingly.

But the real motivation behind the CBDC push is to usurp the financing function from the commercial banks. That's the bigger play. And it would be far more devastating for our economy and our way of life.

This is why the Fed and the New York banks have broken ranks.

Remember, the Fed is a private entity. The New York banking interests were behind its creation in 1913, and they likely own the Fed outright.

So, what we've been watching play out on the world's stage is a battle between very powerful factions. The globalist power structure is on one hand. And the Fed/New York banks are on the other.

This is also why the globalists hate Trump. He's the one who enabled the silent coup to happen at the Fed. I don't know if Trump was a willing player in the plot or if he just unwittingly enabled it, but at the end of the day, it doesn't matter.

A president controlled by the globalist power structure would never have let Jerome Powell and John Williams come to power at the Fed. We'll talk about that more in the next chapter.

But the big takeaway here is that the Fed's aggressive moves to raise interest rates were not about fighting inflation. That was just the cover story.

The reality is that the Fed has orchestrated a well-planned strategy to beat back the globalist power structure. The Fed is fighting for the survival of the New York banks, the commercial banking system itself, and whatever remains of American capitalism.

This is why the Fed never blinked when the UN told it to stop raising rates. And it's why the Fed kept on going even after the US stock market dropped over 20 percent.

Looking forward, this is why the Fed isn't going to "pivot." It hasn't raised rates aggressively just to give itself room to cut later—as so many analysts suggested initially.

To the contrary, the Fed is going to get the Federal Funds Rate back up to what it calls the "terminal" level. This is the rate at which the Fed sees as neutral. That is to say, it's not stimulative nor is it restrictive to the economy.

We don't know what the Fed thinks the terminal rate is. But it's almost certainly between 5 percent and 7 percent.

And all indications are that the Fed is content to get back to the terminal level and then stay put. No more cutting rates drastically every time the stock market hiccups.

If I'm right about this, the days of "easy money" are behind us.

And that means the Age of Paper Wealth is over. The Fed won't backstop the equity markets every time there's a downturn going forward.

I see this battle between the globalist power structure and the Fed/NY banks as the single most important macroeconomic story to watch right now.

If the globalists win, our world will change radically. And not for the better. We'll likely have to rethink everything about our investments and our lifestyle. If the New York banking interests win, we have a shot at getting back to what I guess we can call the "old normal."

Both our economy and our culture have been pretty nutty since 2020. And that's intentional. It was all part of the Great Reset plan. If it's thwarted, perhaps we'll regain a little sanity.

That said, to get a better feel for where we are and the path forward, we have to understand how we got to this position in the first place. That will be the subject of our next chapter.

Key Points

- The banking system today is a "fractional reserve" system
- This system allows banks to issue more loans at a 10:1 ratio relative to their reserves
- The commercial banks help determine which projects get financing and which do not
- The ability to aggregate and allocate capital is critical to modern civilization
- The commercial banking system is highly competitive
- The globalists want to finance uneconomic projects… thus, they must eliminate competition in banking
- CBDCs are about usurping the banking function from the commercial banks
- The Fed and the banks are fighting back with higher rates
- The Age of Paper Wealth is over

Action to take: A great resource to help us understand the current banking system and how it's evolved is Murray Rothbard's *A History of Money and Banking in the United States.* To get a free copy of the e-book, just go to our resources page at: https://beyondthenestegg.com/extras/

CHAPTER THREE

HOW WE GOT HERE

The Fed has spent the last thirty years consistently pumping cheap money into the financial system. By "cheap," I mean money that it created from nothing.

In total, the Fed has created at least $8 trillion. That's what we can verify. And there's a good chance the Fed engineered even more new dollars through back-channels.

This onslaught of money created from nothing drove interest rates down to near-zero.

Then the commercial banks pyramided credit on top of these trillions of dollars by roughly ten-to-one. In other words, for every new dollar created, the banks could lend out ten dollars against it. And remember, this necessarily creates new money from nothing as well.

This all served to create a massive financial bubble in the US and many developed countries around the world.

Meanwhile, major western governments used this funny money to spearhead massive spending programs... for pretty much anything and everything.

The most obvious spending circled around military and welfare-state programs. But a quick search on the private search engine Brave (search.brave.com) for "most ridiculous government spending programs" will reveal all kinds of other shenanigans. It's mind-blowing what these people have done.

As a result, many regular folks have been conditioned to see the government as this great cornucopia. Whenever there's a problem, somehow our society has adopted the idea that it's the government's job to fix it. And given its seemingly infinite resources, the government has been quick to acquiesce.

That's why all western governments are now drowning in debt.

Name any major western country and you can be sure that its debt-to-gross domestic product (GDP) ratio has ballooned in recent decades. In fact, many countries now service a debt that's near or greater than 100 percent of their GDP. To illustrate this, here's an abbreviated list of debt-to-GDP by country as of the end of 2022.[2]

Country	Debt-to-GDP Ratio
Japan	259%
Greece	195%
Singapore	160%
Italy	150%
United States	128%
Portugal	126%
Spain	118%

2 https://worldpopulationreview.com/country-rankings/countries-by-national-debt

Country	Debt-to-GDP Ratio
Canada	113%
France	113%
Belgium	109%
United Kingdom	95%
Brazil	93%

These numbers are unprecedented historically. Never before have so many countries run up a debt that equals or exceeds their gross domestic production.

This is only possible in a world where central banks can create new base money from thin air. And that world has only existed since 1971. That's when US President Richard Nixon removed the dollar's final link to gold.

However, it appears we've reached the limit. We've come to the point where the economy simply cannot handle any more debt and cheap money.

The problem is, there's no easy fix to this mess. The great Austrian economist Ludwig von Mises spelled out the dilemma very clearly in his great work *Human Action: A Treatise on Economics.*

Here's Mises:

There is no means of avoiding the final collapse of a boom brought about by credit expansion. The alternative is only whether the crisis should come sooner as the result of voluntary abandonment of further credit expansion, or later as a final and total catastrophe of the currency system involved.[3]

What Mises was saying is this...

Once you go down the path of manipulating interest rates lower and printing new money from thin air, you necessarily sow the seeds of a future crisis.

If you keep going down that same path for too long, you'll destroy the currency and wreck the economy beyond all recognition. This is the worst-case scenario. But if you recognize that your current trajectory is unsustainable, you can make the decision to reverse course.

This will result in a painful economic contraction. Artificially low interest rates and funny money fuel all kinds of malinvestment, and that malinvestment must be liquidated.

That's what the necessary recession does. It clears out the bad debt and gets rid of unproductive companies. It's not fun to go through, but it's far preferable to destroying the currency and the entire economy.

This is what the battle between the Fed and the globalist power structure is about. The two factions have different preferences for how to move forward.

The globalist elites went all in on their Great Reset plan.

As we discussed, they want to fundamentally restructure the mechanisms of money and credit. They want central banks

---

[3] https://mises.org/library/human-action-0

to be the ultimate arbiter of everything related to finance. And they want these central banks beholden to international organizations that they control.

That is to say, they want to get rid of national sovereignty in everything but name.

That's why they have been trying to attribute arbitrary powers to organizations like the World Health Organization (WHO) and the Centers for Disease Control (CDC). It's all about conditioning the public to see these international organizations as authority figures.

The key is their reset requires the commercial banks to be watered down or eliminated completely. If globalist central banks are to issue all money and credit, there's simply no need for a commercial banking system.

That's why the Fed is fighting back.

Again, the Fed is a private entity. Nobody knows for sure what its aggregated ownership structure looks like.

What we do know is that it was the major New York banking interests who colluded with a prominent US senator to establish the Fed back in 1913. It stands to reason then that the Fed is owned and controlled by the New York banks still today.

That said, former Fed Chairs Ben Bernanke and Janet Yellen are absolutely in league with the globalist power structure. Bernanke's more of a useful academic. But Janet Yellen is viciously and unapologetically in favor of the globalist elites' plot.

So when these two ran the Fed, it catered to globalist interests.

Current Fed Chair Jerome Powell and current head of the Federal Reserve Bank of New York John Williams are clearly in the New York banking fold. That's why President Biden tried to find a convenient excuse to not reappoint Powell for another term in 2021.

I don't know how control of the Fed shifted back from the globalists to the New York banking faction. Perhaps there was an internal struggle. Or perhaps the two simply shared similar interests during the Bernanke and Yellen years.

But what I *do* know is that the New York banks aren't about to give up their commercial banking system. That is precisely why the Fed raised interest rates so aggressively in 2022... when nobody expected them to do so.

Of course, inflation was the cover story. But the Fed didn't raise rates to fight inflation. It was all about draining the Eurodollar market of liquidity. That, in turn, curtails the ECB's ability to finance projects related to the Great Reset.

What's more, the Fed's actions guarantee that we'll have a massive recession in the US and Europe.

Those who can't see what economists call second-order effects will decry this as a bad thing. But recessions aren't bad. They are necessary.

Recessions clear out the bad debt and malinvestment, thus paving the way to a healthy economic recovery—one that enables small business and the middle class to thrive.

To sum it up, there are two ways forward right now. Either we have a reset that wipes away the debt and restructures the entire financial system, or we have a massive recession that clears out the current imbalances and saves the current system.

The globalists prefer option A. The Fed and the New York banks want option B. And because the power, wealth, and influence of each faction hangs in the balance, they are both willing to fight tooth and nail for their plan.

This is going to be a long, drawn-out slugfest. No doubt momentum will shift back and forth at times. But right now, the Fed and the New York banks have the upper hand.

The Fed Will Power Forward

In May 2023 the Federal Funds Rates—the Fed's target interest rate—surpassed 5 percent for the first time in 16 years. The Fed's language made it clear that they did not plan to cut rates anytime soon.

However, the market didn't buy it. Collectively, the market projected that the Fed Funds Rate would fall to 4.1 percent by late 2024.[4]

The problem is, these projections were based on consumer price inflation (CPI) expectations. The market became fixated upon the idea that the Fed would "pivot" and cut rates to stave off a recession.

4 https://www.usatoday.com/story/money/economy/2022/12/14/fed-interest-rate-federal-reserve-meeting-live-updates/10867165002/

But as we've discussed, the Fed isn't going to pivot. It can't.

That's because the Fed and the New York banks need "normalized" interest rates to hold off the globalists and save the commercial banking system.

As we discussed earlier, it appears that we've reached the limits of easy money and near-zero interest rates. Yet governments and markets have become addicted to both.

I suspect the Fed's plan to save the banks is to force fiscal constraints upon everybody once again. I certainly hope that's the case.

Speaking from the American perspective, Congress has been spending money (created from nothing) like a drunken sailor for decades now. Old-fashioned conservatives have been decrying this spending, and the associated debt, for a long time.

But as long as the Fed continued to push rates lower, the debt really didn't matter that much. The debt went up, but debt service costs remained manageable. That's thanks to lower rates.

With rising interest rates, debt service becomes a major problem. That's one reason why so many analysts said the Fed would never raise rates materially.

For every one percent the US government's borrowing costs rise, the government's annual interest payment expense will rise by over $300 billion after the existing debt has been rolled over.

The fact is the vast majority of the US government's $32 trillion debt will have to be rolled over in the coming years. That's because the outstanding Treasury bonds are maturing. If we're right about the Fed not pivoting, either Congress will be forced to cut spending tremendously… or something's going to break in a big way.

I think that there's a good chance that the Fed will remonetize America's gold hoard at some point as well. They will probably have to.

I used to enjoy watching old videos of Dr. Ron Paul grilling Ben Bernanke in Congress. I found Dr. Paul's economic views fascinating.

On one such occasion Paul asked Bernanke why the Fed and the US Treasury still held hundreds of millions of ounces of gold on the balance sheet. Bernanke replied that it was simply "tradition." And he did his best to downplay gold entirely.[5]

Of course, it was all nonsense.

There's a reason why every major government and central bank still owns gold. And that's because it provides them with optionality.

For example, imagine we're in a world where 10-year Treasuries pay 6 percent and the US government has to roll over a significant portion of its national debt.

---

[5] https://www.thestreet.com/markets/commodities/ron-paul-attacks-bernanke-on-gold-11184107

Paying 6 percent on trillions of dollars just isn't doable. The annual interest expense would blow out the budget. But what if the Treasury started to float gold-backed bonds at 3.5 percent instead?

The key is that a certain percentage of the bond would be redeemed in gold at maturity rather than dollars. That's the only way they could get away with offering a lower interest rate.

That's where we're likely headed. To understand this, we must understand how Treasuries work.

When an entity buys a Treasury bond, they are loaning money to the US government. The government pays a rate of return on the bond for its duration, then it repays the entire principal balance at maturity.

As good investors, we understand the Time Value of Money principle. A dollar today is worth more than a dollar tomorrow. This is because the government creates new dollars from nothing every year.

So, if we are investing in Treasuries, we need a strong rate of return to make it worth our while. When they pay us back at maturity, those dollars will buy less than they would have when we originally bought the bond.

But suppose the US government agrees to settle a specific portion of Treasuries in gold. That's gold remonetization. They offer to pay investors back in part with gold.

I doubt that the partial gold backing would be much more than 10 percent, but that's still plenty.

This would allow the Treasury to sell bonds at a much lower rate than they otherwise could. That's thanks to the gold backing. Gold helps protect investors' purchasing power from inflation.

In return, this would allow the government to service the national debt despite rising rates. Debt service costs wouldn't blow up the budget, in other words.

So, we may very well see gold re-monetized in the US and around the world.

In fact, I suspect the BRICS alliance (Brazil, Russia, India, China, South Africa, and others) will go there first. If they do, the US would likely have to follow suit.

The BRICS bloc is furiously developing an international financial system to compete with the existing dollar-based system. Nothing would solidify trust in that system more than some degree of gold backing.

The point is, we're entering an entirely new era here. The Age of Paper Wealth is over.

This is why it is critical that we each develop a robust asset allocation model. Simply pouring all our savings into stocks and funds just won't cut it going forward.

This is also why I advocate developing a cash flow wealth strategy rather than fixating upon capital gains. The days of the Fed backstopping the US equity markets are over. We need a far more comprehensive approach to money and finance than what's been pushed up to this point.

Our approach depends upon which faction wins the ongoing macroeconomic war. That's why this kind of analysis is so critical. And right now, the New York banks appear to have the upper hand.

Davos versus New York

In 2020 the World Economic Forum (WEF) announced its "Great Reset" plan to the world. The WEF is a mouthpiece for the globalist power structure.

If this plan comes to fruition, we'll have to rethink everything about money, finance, and investing. That's why the battle between the globalists and the Fed is so important.

Simply put, this battle has enormous implications for what daily life looks like in the future. And it has equally massive implications on the investment front. That's primarily what we are focusing on in these pages.

For starters, the globalists are aggressively opposed to oil and nuclear energy sources. They claim it's because we're killing the planet. This is where the term "environmental, social, and governance (ESG)" investing came from.

But that's just the cover.

Really, they oppose this traditional energy because it's nearly impossible for them to control. Russia is the primary oil producer in the Eurasian region. Most of the region's uranium deposits (for nuclear fission energy production) are found in Kazakhstan. Those countries are "outsiders" to the globalist faction.

Along the same lines, these people appear to be opposed to our system of individual property rights. That impacts real estate in a big way.

Remember the eviction moratoriums during the Covid hysteria?

Those came from the CDC—an international institution that operates as another mouthpiece for the globalist power structure.

Of course, their call to stop evictions was broadcast far and wide by mainstream news outlets. Basically, they suggested that renters didn't have to pay rent anymore. At least for a while.

Now, we didn't have any issues with this within the real estate network I invest through. Our tenants continued to pay rent as normal. I believe that's largely because we're only investing in localities that have strong property rights protections in place.

Still, this is a clear sign that the people behind the Great Reset are not at all friendly to real estate investors.

Meanwhile, the New York Banking interests have finally denounced ESG investing. The major banks, including JP Morgan CEO Jamie Dimon, are once again calling for greater investment in oil and gas production.[6]

---

6 https://www.bloomberg.com/news/articles/2022-09-21/dimon-defends-need-for-fossil-fuel-investments-to-congress?leadSource=uverify%20wall

At the same time, we know that real estate is a huge boon to the economy and the commercial banking system. As such, the New York banking interests are not at all hostile to real estate investors.

There's evidence of the battle between the New York banks and the globalists everywhere we look. The media won't report it as such, but it's all right there. We just have to read between the lines.

That's why I spend so much time tracking this story. This is the single most important piece of the macroeconomic puzzle. How it shapes up will impact everything related to money and finance and many other aspects of our lives.

Given the choice between the two, those of us who believe in property rights and a market-based system would far prefer the New York banking interests come out on top.

I hold no illusions that somehow these institutions are pure and noble. They aren't. But they do have a vested interest in maintaining whatever's left of America's once-robust capitalist system.

That being the case, I *do* have good news to share. The globalist power structure is on the retreat.

Lessons from Davos 2023

Every year the World Economic Forum hosts an annual conference in Davos, Switzerland. It's usually in January. The conference typically features a smorgasbord of top-tier government officials (past and present) and corporate executives from around the world.

If we look at Davos 2021 and Davos 2022, those events were incredibly upbeat and well-attended. The Covid hysteria was laying the groundwork for their Great Reset perfectly.

If we remember, there were strong calls to eliminate cash, suspend property rights, and to mandate masks and experimental injections at the time. Then a strong censorship culture arose to silence any critical objections or pushback to these items.

To top it off, governments were busy working on several "vaccine passport" systems that would implement draconian travel restrictions around the world.

It lined up perfectly with the Great Reset agenda. That's why Davos was buzzing in 2021 and 2022.

By all accounts, it was the exact opposite in 2023. The mood had completely reversed.

For starters, WEF founder Klaus Schwab wasn't around much at the 2023 conference. He issued the opening remarks but wasn't very active afterward.

In addition, more than a few heads of state declined their invitation to attend. The list includes US president Joe Biden, Canadian president Justin Trudeau, French president Emmanuel Macron, and British prime minister Rishi Sunak.

What's more, leaders of the Covid hysteria Anthony Fauci and Bill Gates also declined to attend, as did prominent globalist financier George Soros.[7]

There's an old saying that comes to mind. It goes, "The darkness cannot survive the light."

The point is, very few people knew that the World Economic Forum even existed a few years ago. As such, the WEF was able to operate with the luxury of being out of public sight.

Today, thanks to independent media, millions of people are aware of the WEF and what it's up to. As such, I suspect the prominent figures who declined to attend Davos in 2023 did so because they knew it would further damage their reputation.

In other words, the light is now shining. As it turns out, most people don't like the idea of a small group of power brokers dictating major changes to their society and their way of life.

To me, lighter attendance for Davos 2023 was a very strong sign that the Great Reset plan hit a major snag. And there's additional supporting evidence as well…

Morgan Stanley CEO James Gorman went on Bloomberg a few weeks after Davos 2023. He said that the World Economic Forum was nothing more than an echo chamber. He called it a place where "everybody's basically repeating back to each other what they've heard from the last person."[8]

---

7 https://www.politico.eu/article/davos-world-economic-forum-guest-list-politics-business/

8 https://www.zerohedge.com/economics/morgan-stanley-ceo-says-inflation-clearly-peaked-decries-davos-echo-chamber

We hadn't seen such sharp criticism of the WEF in the financial media before.

Meanwhile, ESG champion and WEF lackey Larry Fink, the CEO of investment management giant BlackRock, was forced to go on a media campaign of his own. Fink had to get on camera and defend ESG investing. He tried very hard to assure the financial community that BlackRock was not in any financial trouble.[9]

This isn't something executives do when everything is going well. In fact, I remember Lehman Brothers CEO Dick Fuld having to make similar media appearances in the months leading up to Lehman's collapse.

Despite Fink's plea, BlackRock's investors scrambled to pull their money out of its funds. It caused such a hit that BlackRock had to limit withdrawals to just 0.3 percent of net assets. The firm also floated the idea of raising additional money to cover withdrawal requests.[10]

So it looks like the New York banking interests gained an upper hand in the battle. The globalist powers and their allies were forced to pull back on their plans.

But here's the thing—even if the New York banks save the current system, we still aren't going back to the days of easy money. We'll talk about why in the next chapter.

---

9 https://www.cnbc.com/video/2023/01/13/pro-watch-cnbcs-full-interview-with-blackrock-ceo-larry-fink.html

10 https://www.reuters.com/business/finance/blackstone-limits-redemptions-69-billion-reit-2022-12-01/

Key Points

- The Fed, the commercial banks, and the Treasury created a massive financial bubble in the US and around the world
- This financed enormous government spending programs and drove debt-to-GDP ratios through the roof
- The problem is, we've reached the limit
- As Mises pointed out, there are only two choices—continue to inflate and destroy the currency or allow a recession to clear out the bad debt
- The globalist elites want to continue to inflate and implement their Great Reset
- The New York banks want to allow a recession and save the current system
- To accomplish their ends, the Fed and the New York banks need to "normalize" interest rates
- As rates rise, the US government's debt becomes harder to service
- That means Congress will have to cut spending… or something will break
- Gold remonetization is possible within the current climate
- The BRICs block will likely remonetize gold first… the US will follow
- The Age of Paper Wealth is over, and we need a more comprehensive approach to money and finance to account for this

CHAPTER FOUR

THE FED PIVOT ALREADY HAPPENED

Most of the world is in the dark about what the Federal Reserve has been up to.

What the world sees is a reactionary institution that had to grapple with consumer price inflation by raising interest rates. That certainly makes for a great cover story, but the reality is much more nuanced.

With a little more detailed analysis, it becomes quite clear that the Fed's aggressive rate hikes weren't really about inflation. Instead, the Fed acted to save the commercial banking system as it currently exists. One could make the case that this is an effort to save the last vestiges of American capitalism as well.

Now, please know that my analysis here is based on what we used to call the Scientific Method. That was in the pre-Covid days, when "the Science" wasn't a deity to be worshiped.

The Scientific Method involves doing extensive research into a given topic and then forming a hypothesis. Then you test your hypothesis to see if it holds up.

And objectivity is the key here.

Testing a hypothesis requires you to honestly look for ways in which it may be wrong. It's the opposite of the social media echo chambers where people are only trying to validate their pre-existing beliefs.

The longer your hypothesis holds up to real-world data, the more confident you can be that it holds merit. That doesn't necessarily mean that it's completely correct. Just that it hasn't been proven wrong.

It was early in 2022 when my research led me to the hypothesis that I've presented to you in these pages. The idea that the Fed and the New York banks broke ranks from the globalist power structure that rotates around Europe and the European Central Bank (ECB).

My confidence in this hypothesis has increased with every month that's passed since. It continues to hold up to real world data. Certain events have even seemed to confirm it more tangibly.

For those of us who are of the Austrian school persuasion when it comes to economic analysis, this statement may seem conflicting. After all, the Fed's very creation in 1913 was a coup against free markets.

The Fed's job description is to manipulate interest rates and centrally plan monetary policy. These are two functions that should be left to the market in a pure capitalist system.

Plus, the Fed seemingly worked hand-in-hand with the US government and the globalist power structure going back at least to the early 1980s.

Fed Chair Ben Bernanke's actions while manning the helm at the Fed from 2006 to 2014 certainly enabled the Bush and Obama administrations' globalist-leaning big-government, big-spending agendas. Then Janet Yellen took over in 2014 and continued the same easy money policies.

In total, the Fed monetized nearly $3.6 trillion worth of government debt from 2006 to 2018—the year Yellen left the Fed. In other words, the Fed created $3.6 trillion from thin air to finance increased government spending in that time.

We can see this clearly in the following chart:

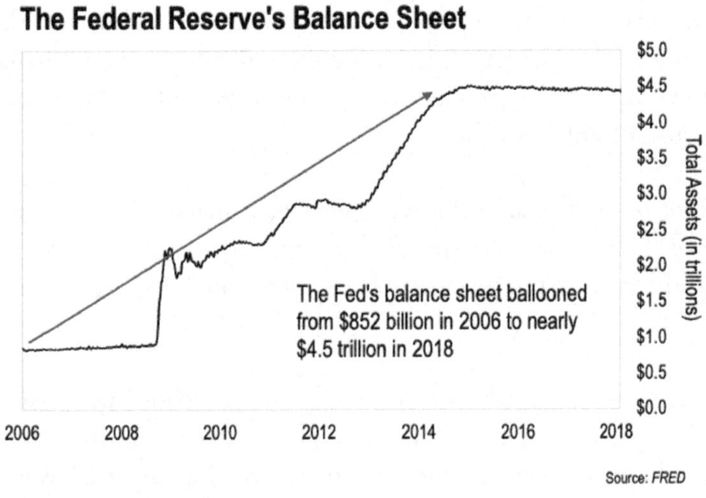

Here we can see the total assets held on the Federal Reserve's balance sheet through the Bernanke and Yellen years.[11] What's important to understand is that when the line goes up, that's the Fed creating new dollars to finance government spending.

[11] https://fred.stlouisfed.org/series/WALCL

Then Jerome Powell replaced Janet Yellen as Fed Chair in 2018, and it looked like he was just another interchangeable piece.

Well, to be fair, Powell did shrink the Fed's balance sheet from over $4.4 trillion in 2018 to just about $3.7 trillion in 2019. This had the effect of sucking dollars out of the system, which tends to put upward pressure on interest rates and downward pressure on stock prices.

When the US equity markets began selling off, Powell immediately reversed course—just like his predecessors had done before him. What's more, Powell's Fed monetized nearly $5 trillion in government spending in response to the COVID-19 episode.[12] Again, this was new money created from thin air.

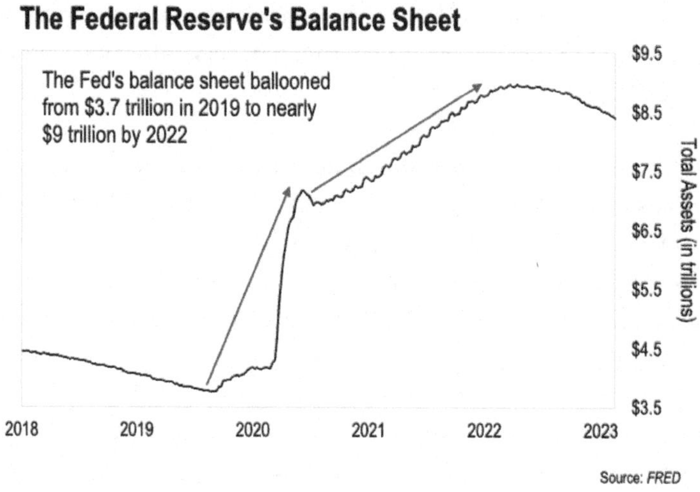

It certainly looked like Powell's Fed was no different from Bernanke and Yellen's.

---

12 https://fred.stlouisfed.org/series/WALCL

He even went on national television in April 2021 and assured the nation that consumer price inflation would be transitory. That's despite the massive helicopter drop of new money into the system.

It wasn't until 2022 that Powell began to signal that the easy money days were over. That was the Fed pivot.

Reading between the lines, Powell made it very clear that he no longer wanted to enable infinite government spending. Nor did he want to backstop the US equity markets anymore. That is to say, he suggested that the Fed Put was dead, albeit indirectly.

The Fed Put refers to the fact that the Fed has historically cut interest rates and pumped easy money into the financial system every time the US equity markets faced a meaningful correction. This helped juice the markets and push stock prices higher once again.

Of course, nobody paid much attention to Powell's hawkish signals in 2022. Four decades of falling interest rates and loose monetary policy led the markets to believe that these easy money policies were permanent—debt, deficits, and zombie companies be damned. We'll talk about this more in a few minutes.

But because of the historical precedent, every time Powell raised rates, most analysts just repeated the same popular assessment to one another—Powell was raising rates in the present to fight inflation. And they also agreed that he would pivot and cut rates once again when consumer price inflation subsided.

The implication was that as soon as the Fed pivot came, the stock market would be off to the races and we'd be right back where we were in 2021.

I believe those analysts allowed their bias to blind them to what was playing out before their eyes.

Simply put, the Fed pivot happened in 2022. The real pivot was Powell's move away from easy money policies and back to some form of fiscal sanity.

Powell's Fed is moving us back to a world in which we have "normal" interest rates. A world where governments and corporations can't borrow trillions and trillions of dollars without consequence.

I think Powell's actions speak for themselves here. But it was a great interview with Danielle DiMartino Booth early in 2023 that essentially confirmed much of this thesis for me.

Confirmed - the Fed Put is Dead

Danielle DiMartino Booth is both a Wall Street veteran and a Fed insider. She began her career on Wall Street, and then she spent nine years at the Federal Reserve Bank of Dallas. There, she served as an advisor to Dallas Fed President Richard Fisher.

Today DiMartino Booth is the founder and CEO of a research firm called Quill Intelligence. And she still has some connections within the Federal Reserve System. Those connections give her a more nuanced understanding of what's happening behind closed doors at the Eccles Building.[13]

Booth's interview that caught my attention was on Tom Luongo's Gold, Goats, and Guns podcast.[14] And I highly recommend it. Tom's work has heavily influenced my own thinking on these matters.

In that interview Booth made it clear that there tends to be a bureaucratic echo chamber at the lower levels of the Fed. Here's what that means…

We see the Fed Chair when they go on television and when they are quoted in news articles. But what we don't see is the underlying team of people who feed research and analysis to the Chair. That team tends to consist primarily of academic researchers.

According to Booth, Powell's comments on inflation being transitory in 2021 were based on the analysis he received from academic researchers within the Fed.

Obviously that analysis was completely wrong. It left Powell with "egg on his face," as Booth put it in the interview.

She went on to explain that this incident woke Powell up to the fact that there was an academic echo chamber within the Fed. Ever since then Powell has been looking to "outside" data and analysis to guide his decisions.

---

13 https://quillintelligence.com/

14 https://podcasts.apple.com/us/podcast/episode-133-danielle-dimartino-booth-and-why-the-fed/id1435023391?i=1000599571148

Now, Booth didn't elaborate on this point, but I think it's a safe assumption to say that this "outside" analysis has come from Powell's network within the upper echelon of the New York banking scene.

This could explain why Powell seemed to continue Bernanke and Yellen's policies in his first few years as Fed Chair… and why he seemingly did an about-face in 2022.

This also lends credence to the hypothesis that the Fed and the New York banks have broken ranks with the globalist power structure. And Booth provided us with more supporting evidence of this. She did so by pointing out what sets Powell apart from Bernanke and Yellen.

The latter were both purely academics. They had no real-world experience within the financial markets.

I'm reading between the lines a little bit here, but Booth seemingly suggested that Bernanke was something of an "empty suit" academic. She didn't use those exact words, of course. But she somewhat implied that he simply went along with whatever academic research was popular at the time. And that research was driven by the globalist narrative that's been so popular within the establishment.

Booth also implied that Yellen, while purely an academic, is also something of an idealogue.

Yellen fervently believes that the global elite know what's best when it comes to how to manage society and keep the common folk in line. Those are my words, but Booth's comments seem to support that idea.

Jerome Powell's different. Booth reminded us that he's not an academic. Powell was a Wall Street veteran. He had direct experience within the financial markets.

What's more, Powell made a fortune on Wall Street. He built a net worth in excess of $100 million.

That also sets him apart from Bernanke and Yellen. They both made their money *after* becoming Fed Chair.

So, we should ask the important question: what motivates Jerome Powell? What are his incentives?

For Bernanke and Yellen, they knew they would get paid handsomely if they did what the establishment wanted them to do. Book deals… six and seven figure speaking fees… overpriced consultations—there are plenty of ways to reward lackeys for good behavior.

But Powell doesn't need their money. So, what's he after here?

Booth offered her opinion directly. She thinks that Powell sees himself as serving his country.

She also explained that Powell was very critical of the Fed's prolonged zero-bound interest rate policy. He tried to warn Fed officials that the longer they kept rates at zero, the harder it would be to unwind that policy.

At that point in the interview Luongo interjected with a thought: If Powell was critical of existing Fed policy, why did he enable all the reckless spending in response to the Covid hysteria?

Then Tom also shared *his* theory. He thinks that the Biden administration basically forced the Fed to monetize their Covid response policies. They intentionally rushed everything through at the height of the panic.

Given the media's "flooding the zone" fear campaign, Luongo thinks that Powell had no choice but to monetize the $5 trillion in government spending. His entire staff would turn on him if he didn't.

Booth didn't comment on this theory at all. She didn't confirm it, nor did she debunk it. We can take that for what it's worth.

What she did say is that Powell was always dead set on killing the Fed Put. He planned to raise rates back up to a reasonable level regardless of what happened to stock prices.

It's all a balance between enabling economic activity and discouraging the rampant speculation and wasteful spending that's been happening for many years now. Booth specifically said that Powell wanted to put an end to "malinvestment."

Now, I have to emphasize again that this is why the Fed is so problematic as an institution. By intervening in the markets, it has created a very tenuous dynamic that would not exist if money and interest rates were left to market forces.

In other words, the Fed itself encouraged decades of malinvestment. Now Powell wants to reverse course.

This certainly supports my belief that the Fed isn't going to back down from its hawkish stance. There will be no pivot back to cheap money and low interest rates.

Finally, DiMartino Booth made a somewhat emotionally charged comment toward the end of the interview. She said that there will be an American central bank digital currency (CBDC) "over Powell's dead body."

According to Booth, Powell's Fed will do everything it can to make sure that our CBDC is nothing more than a back-end settlement mechanism. A 'wholesale' CBDC. It will simply be a replacement for the antiquated SWIFT system.

From my perspective, this is all good news.

It appears the New York banks want to get back to some semblance of fiscal responsibility. This includes normal interest rates that reward savers and discourage malinvestment.

Of course, this means all the malinvestment that's happened over the last decade-plus will need to be liquidated. Which in turn means that some assets will be repriced and a bunch of zombie companies will likely go under. That's going to be an ugly process.

At the same time, there will be some tremendous opportunities as this process plays out. The key here is that there's now a path forward to a new American renaissance—believe it or not.

Everybody is out there cursing the Fed for its aggressive rate-hiking campaign, but they are missing the big picture. The Fed is forcing fiscal responsibility upon the system once again.

As Mises pointed out, there are only two ways to get out of zero-bound rates and cheap money policies: voluntary abandonment or total collapse of the monetary system.

The fact is, we embarked upon the path of zero-bound interest rates and funny money in 2008. This created an incredible bull market in US equities because funny money always feeds speculative booms.

But the buck stopped in 2022. That's when the Fed decided to choose Mises' voluntary abandonment option.

Again, this doesn't mean the Fed is "good." It's simply acting in its own best interest.

What we need to understand as investors is that normalizing rates is the path back to a healthy economy. That's what's happening here. But we're going to have to endure a recession first. That's unavoidable.

Still, a recession doesn't change the fact that we're staring down the barrel of a new American renaissance. In fact, it's what will clear the path. If we realize this, there are incredible investment opportunities available to us every step of the way.

Now I want to interject a little disclaimer here...

Please don't mistake any of this as fanfare or explicit cheerleading for the Fed or the banks. It's just my analysis.

I'm 100 percent in the Austrian camp. And the great Austrian economists have convinced me that our economy would operate more efficiently and more equitably without a central bank and without a fractional reserve banking system. I don't waver on that.

At the same time, all we can do right now is operate within the system that we have. And I absolutely believe the system we have today is far preferable to what the globalist elites would like to replace it with.

As the old saying goes, don't let perfect be the enemy of good. Or perhaps in this case we shouldn't let 'ideal' be the enemy of 'functional.'

The bottom line is this—the approach to asset allocation and rental real estate that we suggest will remain viable in the years to come so long as the Fed and the New York banks fend off the globalist elites. And fortunately, that appears to be exactly what's happening.

Now that we have a feel for what's happening on the macroeconomic stage, let's shift our focus to finance and investing. We'll start with the lesson from Monopoly—that's the subject of our next chapter.

Key Points

- The financial world hasn't yet realized what the Fed is really doing
- The Fed's rate hikes were never about inflation… they were about saving the current system
- Applying the Scientific Method to this thesis
- The Fed's actions, in hindsight
- Confirmed—the Fed Put is dead
- The difference between Jerome Powell and his predecessors
- Powell is explicitly opposed to a retail CBDC
- The Fed is choosing Mises' voluntary abandonment option
- We're staring down the barrel of a new American renaissance

CHAPTER FIVE

THE LESSON FROM MONOPOLY

As I mentioned at the beginning of this book, financial independence is my passion. That's what drives me. But I don't approach this from a consumerist perspective. I care little for cars, luxuries, and material goods.

To me, the true purpose of money is to acquire assets. That's the key lesson in the classic board game *Monopoly*. If we acquire assets, then we will always have the financial means to take care of ourselves and our families, even if our active income were to go away.

If we accept that statement as true, the only remaining question becomes: what assets should we acquire?

This is where we run into the information problem again. If we go online and search for investment ideas and strategies, we are overwhelmed by an absolute avalanche of what I call piecemeal investment advice. These are one-off investment ideas that aren't part of any overarching system or strategy.

There are plenty of services that focus on buying stocks or bonds in a particular sector or market. There are also scores of trading systems out there. They all promise to help us line our pockets with big gains.

To be sure, some of these services are decent, but none of them provide a *comprehensive* approach to finance. They don't provide a fully integrated system for becoming financially independent, nor do they help us implement a complimentary tax strategy to maximize our investment returns. Most of the time, they'll keep mum on the tax issue just for liability purposes.

I spent the first ten years of my professional life chasing these kinds of piecemeal investments. I would stumble upon a few stock ideas that I liked, so I would buy them. Then I would hear about a great set-up in the corporate bond space, so I would buy it. Then I would learn about a new approach to trading options, so I would try it out.

As a result, I was always bouncing from one thing to another. There was no structure or system to it—and taxes were an afterthought. When it came time to file my tax return, I just hoped for the best.

Perhaps it's no surprise then that after ten years, I still hadn't made much progress toward financial independence. Sure, I made a little money on a few of the ideas that I had pursued, but that was typically offset by losing money in other areas. And because I didn't have a tax strategy in place, one year I found myself having to dip into my individual retirement account (IRA) early. I took out a sizeable withdrawal to cover myself, then the Internal Revenue Service (IRS) hit me with a 10 percent early withdrawal fee for my efforts. I had to pay income taxes *and* a big penalty on the money I removed. You just can't get financially independent by making mistakes like that.

Needless to say, I didn't start to see any real financial results until I wisened up.

It started with an honest and thorough assessment of the monetary system and the macroeconomic climate. Gaining that understanding enabled me to build a robust asset allocation model.

We'll talk about this concept a lot more in the next chapter, but in essence, asset allocation is all about financial security. It's about strategically allocating capital to a wide range of assets. Cash, gold, stocks, bonds, real estate, Bitcoin, and early-stage investments are the main assets on my radar.

This is true diversity—we're going to talk more on that later, as well.

The key here is that our asset allocation model becomes our reserve. We can instantly turn these assets into cash in the event of an emergency. They are our safety net.

However, our asset portfolio is *not* our retirement savings. In fact, I reject the idea of retirement entirely.

Think about it this way. The traditional approach to retirement promotes the "nest egg" model, the idea that we need to pour our savings into financial assets to work up to this mythical retirement number. "*What's Your Number?*" I remember old commercials promoting that slogan.

The idea was that we would build financial assets and hope our returns get us up to a big enough number that we can live comfortably in retirement. Then, we draw down our assets to create income for ourselves after we quit working. That is to say, we sell off our stocks and funds and use that money to live.

Notice how it's always a choice between assets and income? When our assets are going up, we don't have the income. Then when we want the income, our assets have to come down.

And it gets worse.

This approach pits us against the tax code. It doesn't matter if our financial assets are in 401(k)s, IRAs, or regular brokerage accounts—they are going to get taxed in the end, and tax rates are likely to go up in the coming years. That would not surprise me.

I'd like to use an example to illustrate just how fragile this is. Let's assume we work up to one million dollars, just for easy numbers. We get to retirement with a million-dollar nest egg—plus, we have a little Social Security money coming in. So we say, "You know what, I want to draw $70,000 a year from my nest egg to live comfortably. That will supplement my Social Security."

Keep in mind, to get that $70,000 we have to sell our financial assets. And *that* means we will have to pay taxes on the proceeds.

Now, let's assume we have a conservative tax rate of 15 percent to work with. At that rate, we have to sell about $83,000 worth of assets to get our $70,000 in income for the year. The other $13,000 goes to taxes.

To keep our example here simple, let's assume our tax rate never changes. If we run the numbers, that means we can sell $83,000 worth of assets each year for exactly twelve years. That's it. After twelve years, we are out of money. And the more we draw down our assets, the more fragile our situation becomes.

But wait a minute! Sharp readers may point out that I'm assuming no return on investment in this example. That's correct. But I have bad news for you—it doesn't get much better.

Let's suppose we can generate a consistent 4 percent annual return on our $1 million nest egg. If we can pull this off—without having any down years—then we'll only have gone through about half our nest egg after ten years.

Then we'll have seven more years to burn through the rest. By year 16 we'll only have $72,000 left. By year 17, we're completely broke.

The following graphic shows the calculations:

Year	Deposits & Withdrawals	Interest	Total Deposits & Withdrawals	Accrued Interest	Balance
0	$1,000,000.00	–	$1,000,000.00	–	**$1,000,000.00**
1	($83,000.00)	$40,741.54	$917,000.00	$40,741.54	**$957,741.54**
2	($83,000.00)	$39,019.87	$834,000.00	$79,761.41	**$913,761.41**
3	($83,000.00)	$37,228.05	$751,000.00	$116,989.46	**$867,989.46**
4	($83,000.00)	$35,363.23	$668,000.00	$152,352.69	**$820,352.69**
5	($83,000.00)	$33,422.43	$585,000.00	$185,775.13	**$770,775.13**
6	($83,000.00)	$31,402.57	$502,000.00	$217,177.69	**$719,177.69**
7	($83,000.00)	$29,300.41	$419,000.00	$246,478.10	**$665,478.10**
8	($83,000.00)	$27,112.60	$336,000.00	$273,590.71	**$609,590.71**
9	($83,000.00)	$24,835.67	$253,000.00	$298,426.37	**$551,426.37**
10	($83,000.00)	$22,465.96	$170,000.00	$320,892.33	**$490,892.33**
11	($83,000.00)	$19,999.71	$87,000.00	$340,892.04	**$427,892.04**
12	($83,000.00)	$17,432.98	$4,000.00	$358,325.03	**$362,325.03**
13	($83,000.00)	$14,761.68	($79,000.00)	$373,086.71	**$294,086.71**
14	($83,000.00)	$11,981.55	($162,000.00)	$385,068.25	**$223,068.25**
15	($83,000.00)	$9,088.14	($245,000.00)	$394,156.40	**$149,156.40**
16	($83,000.00)	$6,076.86	($328,000.00)	$400,233.26	**$72,233.26**
17	($83,000.00)	$2,942.89	($411,000.00)	$403,176.15	**($7,823.85)**

To be fair, we'll be far more comfortable with our finances for a little while in this scenario. That's because our nest egg will produce over $20,000 a year in interest income for us for 10 years.

But do you notice how it snowballs in the wrong direction after that? It quickly gets to the point where we can't afford any emergencies. We can't afford to do anything but try to maintain our standard of living. If you think this makes little to no sense, you aren't the only one. Especially not because I *know* that there's a better way.

If all we are really trying to do here is make sure we have enough income to live on in retirement, why take the roundabout way to income? Why not just build the income streams in our working years?

I believe the traditional approach puts us on an unstable see-saw. We constantly have to choose between having assets or having income.

Personally, I would rather have assets and income. And I would like my income to go up when my assets go up. I want the two on the same team.

The good news is that this is absolutely attainable. And it's far more simple than many realize. The key is to acquire assets that produce income. This will let us put assets and income on the same team. When our assets go up, so does our income.

Then, when we want more income, we just buy more assets. It's a far more robust approach.

And guess what? We're no longer talking about traditional retirement here.

If we can work up to having monthly income that supports all our needs and wants... Well, we can retire any time we want. It doesn't matter if we are 65 or 45. All we have to do is build up the income.

So, what about taxes?

This is why I see real estate—old-fashioned rental real estate—as the best vehicle for building income.

Real estate is an incredibly tax-advantaged asset. By default, we shouldn't owe any taxes on our rental income.

That's because for every property we buy, the IRS says we can "depreciate" a fixed percentage of its total value every year.

In other words, we can write off a portion of the property's value against our income every year, even though we didn't lose the money.

Depreciation is a phantom loss. It's used solely for tax purposes.

And that's just *one* element to it.

When we talk about investing in real estate, we're really talking about building a business. So we run everything through LLCs. Then we take into account the tax deductions available to us.

Home office expenses... subscription fees... educational resources... we can write off anything that we buy for our business for tax purposes. This includes expenses that we may have incurred anyway.

For example, my wife and I partner on some rental properties. We are each 50 percent owners of the LLC that owns these properties. Like many married couples, we like to go out to a nice dinner every now and then.

Going out to eat is something that we would do no matter what. But because we spend much of our dinners talking about our real estate business, those dinners are in fact business meetings. And business meetings are tax deductible.

To determine if something is deductible, the Internal Revenue Service (IRS) says that it must be ordinary and necessary for the business. And it must serve a true business purpose.

Well, it's certainly necessary for co-owners in a business to have regular meetings. And having those meetings take place over dinner once a month is certainly ordinary. In fact, most businesses use lunch and dinner meetings routinely.

Here's the thing though—if my wife and I started going out to dinner several times a week… at some point we aren't talking about business meetings any more. It is not ordinary or necessary for most businesses to have multiple dinner meetings every week.

So we only go out to dinner once a month. Then we write it off. It's really that easy.

The point is, the tax code is actually very reasonable. Now, that doesn't mean I agree with all of it. It just means that it's not difficult to do everything by the book.

Here's the best part—if we do everything by the book, we will almost certainly not owe any taxes on our rental income. That's how much the tax code favors real estate.

And it can get far more advanced than that. There are ways to create massive paper losses to offset other sources of income. Again, all by the book. Doing this takes advanced tax planning and a good CPA, but it's possible.

The bottom line here is that when we start talking about creating extra income using rental real estate, it's not like the nest-egg approach where we get hit with taxes every time we want to access our money.

Quite the opposite, actually. What we're talking about is completely tax-free money.

Let's compare the income approach to the nest-egg approach using the same example from above.

Remember, we decided that we want to have an annual income of $70,000 to live comfortably in retirement. By the way, this is just for example purposes. I don't mean to imply that $70,000 is the magic number.

As we explored earlier, if we have a financial nest egg of one million dollars, we have to sell $83,000 worth of assets a year to end up with $70,000 after taxes to live on. And we can do this for twelve to 16 years before we run out of money.

But what happens if we spent our working years buying real estate that provides monthly cash flow for us?

Let's assume that we spend our time buying single family properties that produce, on average, $600 a month in cash flow. That's $7,200 a year per property.

In this case all we need is ten properties to have an extra $72,000 in annual income. That's it.

This is something that's fully within the grasp of anyone. At least if they have the right resources and network. We'll talk about that a lot more later.

And guess what?

These ten properties are going to crank out that $72,000 a year for us indefinitely. Meanwhile, our friends who built a $1 million nest egg will quickly tear through their savings in retirement.

Do you see the magic here? Focusing on income is simply a better way to go.

Hopefully, I made it all sound simple. Because it is.

Of course, that doesn't mean it's easy. Real estate is a slow game at first. It takes some discipline to get started with it. But what it doesn't take is luck. Not when we buy real estate right, anyway.

And remember, we focus on real estate only after we have a solid asset allocation model in place. That way we always have reserves to fall back on in case of emergency.

Put it all together and we've got a system that can create financial independence for us in a relatively short period of time. Our real estate cash flow will rise to the point where it replaces our active income.

At that point we aren't dependent upon a job or an active business for income any longer. We can spend our time doing only those things that are meaningful to us. If we're good stewards, we can use our independence to be of tremendous service to our family, friends, and communities. That's my passion.

Of course, this approach only works if we are allocating the right amount to the right assets… and if we are buying the right real estate in the right markets. That's what we'll discuss in the chapters to come.

Key Points

- The true purpose of money is to acquire assets—this is the lesson of *Monopoly*
- Assets are what provide us with financial security
- Be wary of "piecemeal" investment advice
- Asset allocation enables true diversity
- The traditional "nest egg" model is fragile... and it pits us against the tax code
- Building passive income streams is a better way to plan for retirement
- Rental real estate is a tax-advantaged path to passive income
- Working up to $70,000 a year in passive income is not difficult with real estate
- Financial independence empowers us to be good stewards

Action to take: A great resource to help us understand the current monetary system is Episode One of Mike Maloney's *Hidden Secrets of Money* series. To access the video, just go to our resources page at: https://beyondthenestegg.com/extras/

CHAPTER SIX

ASSET ALLOCATION

Let's get this chapter started with a brief overview of asset allocation. The concept is simple but incredibly important.

Asset allocation is about spreading our money—our capital—across several different asset classes. I find it's best to do this according to a personalized model. The purpose here is true diversification.

I suspect many of us hear the word diversification and CNBC's definition comes to mind. You know, buy stocks in all kinds of different industries so that we have a diversified portfolio.

I don't believe that.

Whenever we see market crashes or bear markets, they typically take all stocks down. Maybe utility stocks go down less than early-stage biotech stocks… but they go down all the same.

Asset allocation is about true diversification. Stocks are just one piece of the model. This way, if the stock market takes a hit, we don't have all our eggs in that basket. We've got other assets to fall back on.

I see asset allocation as a conservative financial strategy. It's all about building the base—the foundation. And once it's built, we can then dial in on an aggressive wealth strategy that will focus on building extra income sources for us.

The reason why we don't start with an aggressive wealth strategy—we start with asset allocation—is because our wealth strategy will focus on income-producing assets that are typically not liquid.

If we run into an emergency where we need to raise cash to pay for something, we need to have liquid assets to fall back on. That's why asset allocation is so important. It provides us with true financial security.

So here's what this looks like. An antifragile Asset Allocation Model will consist of:

- 10–20% Cash
- 5–20% Precious metals
- 10–50% Real estate
- 10–20% Stocks
- 0–10% Bonds
- 5–20% Bitcoin and digital assets
- 0–5% Early-stage investments

These are my suggested ranges for each asset class listed. Keep in mind this model is just a suggestion.

Your own allocation ratio is going to depend upon your personal circumstances and what the macro economic environment happens to look like at any given time.

Personally, I have a running spreadsheet I use to keep track of my own asset allocation model. It's similar to a personal financial statement, but it compares my actual allocation in each asset class to my target allocation at all times.

For example, if the price of gold or Bitcoin falls, it may push my allocation in each below my target level. That's my signal to buy more to bring my allocation back into range.

In a sense, this is a very simple market-timing indicator. And that's all we need for our purposes. Remember, asset allocation is about security. It's not about trying to hit it big on any one investment.

This brings up the obvious question—in what order should we build out our model? If we're just getting started, which assets should we focus on first?

The answer is cash. The first thing we should do is build 6–12 months' worth of a cash reserve. That's where we start.

After that the order is really a matter of preference and where the markets happen to be trading.

If it were me, I would build out my Bitcoin and my gold allocation before delving into the stock market, assuming normal market conditions. However, if the stock market has been beaten up and individual stocks are trading at terrific valuations, then it may make sense to focus on stocks first.

Once your cash allocation is in place, it doesn't matter too much which order you build up your other assets. We should approach it as a marathon, not a sprint.

And keep in mind that more specific guidance is absolutely available to you.

At the end of this chapter, I'll show you how to download our asset allocation spreadsheet template. I would also like to point out that we offer personalized guidance within our investment membership, *The Phoenician League.*

Among many other features, *The Phoenician League* specializes in working with members to craft a customized asset allocation model. We also provide comprehensive training on how to invest in each asset class.

What's more, we maintain a list of actionable stock and early-stage investments for members. We track these suggestions daily. And we provide an update on each of them in our monthly newsletter.

Our goal is to take all the guesswork and gruntwork out of building financial security and ultimately financial independence. We also have a tight-knit community in place where we support one another and discuss new ideas and strategies as well.

I'll provide you with a link to our membership page at the end of this chapter if you're interested in learning more about *The Phoenician League.*

A Word on Alternative Investments

Now that we have a thorough understanding of asset allocation, and the various assets that should be used to build our model, we have to talk about some alternative investments. These are investments that exist outside of our asset allocation model but which are still important to consider.

The first thing that I want to address here is what I call *home resiliency.*

I have practiced and preached this concept for over a decade now. For the longest time it didn't seem very important. In fact, some considered it kind of weird. Then COVID-19 happened in 2020, and it suddenly became evident why this is so important.

Home resiliency refers to the ability to be self-sufficient for at least six months within our home. That means we have all the food, water, and provisions we need to get by and maybe even live comfortably—even if we can't leave our house or receive any deliveries.

The idea here is that we want the ability to "wait out" any emergency or supply chain disruption for at least six months.

When you're just getting started, this seems like a daunting task. But it's actually fairly simple to achieve. And it doesn't cost that much.

Home resiliency consists of four parts—food, water, energy, and provisions. Please note, I'm using provisions as a blanket term for everything that we use regularly that's not food or water, from paper towels to cleaners and everything in between.

Let's start with food...

The easiest way to build a food reserve is to buy pre-packaged food with a long shelf life. There are numerous companies out there that offer suitable products.

Mountain House, Wise Company, Augason Farms, Legacy Food Storage, My Patriot Supply, Thrive Life, and ReadWise each offer various food storage packages.

Keep in mind this is food specifically designed to have a long shelf life. It may not taste the best, and it may not be the most nutritious, but it'll get us by in a pinch.

So if our home resiliency goal is to be self-sufficient for up to six months, the easiest thing to do is to buy six months' worth of stored food.

In addition, I like to keep some extra canned goods, rice, and peanut butter in the pantry as well. Just in case. We also keep our meat freezer stocked at all times.

Next up is water.

Water's a bit more difficult to store because you don't want it sitting in direct light for too long. Plus it takes up a fair amount of space. But I've got a pretty good solution here.

Water.com offers monthly and bi-weekly water delivery services. We can set up a subscription to receive five-gallon jugs of water from that site. Then a service representative will come out to our house every two weeks to bring us new jugs.

I started by buying 15 five-gallon jugs of water. Typically we go through three or four jugs every two weeks. Then when the service rep comes out, he simply replaces our empty jugs.

As such, we have anywhere from 55 to 75 gallons of water on hand at all times. We just drink it as we go and have our service rep replenish our stash every two weeks.

The key here is to store the water out of direct sunlight and to be diligent with a rotation system, to ensure that your water never stagnates. In addition, we keep eight or ten cases of bottled water in the closet at all times. They supplement our five-gallon jugs.

We also collect rain water… just in case. There are quite a few rain-collection kits available on Amazon.com. They consist of a big barrel that can redirect water from one of our home's gutters.

By combining all of these sources, we should have more than enough water to be completely self-sufficient for at least six months.

The next thing we need to think about is energy. We need something that provides heat and enables us to cook in case the power's out during an emergency.

The easiest thing here is to buy a propane grill or two. We have a large one and one of the small portable grills. And we keep a few extra propane tanks on hand at all times. Easy and simple.

I also love having a wood-burning stove. That's not going to be an option for some people, but if you're in a place where it's feasible, a wood stove means you can always cook and heat the house, so long as you have wood to burn.

And the easiest way to get wood is to buy it from somebody locally. I'd wager most towns have numerous people who sell firewood on the side. We just have to ask around a little bit to find them.

Propane grills and a wood stove should provide us with at least six months' worth of energy self-sufficiency.

The other thing I highly recommend are solar-compatible batteries. We keep a few of these around the house, fully charged at all times.

These are batteries that can be charged by plugging them into the wall or hooking them into the solar panel they come with. The Jackery brand is probably the most popular of these products. The batteries are equipped with power outlets that work the same as our wall outlets. Thus, we can plug any electronic device into them to get power.

They would be good for powering any electronic device for a limited period of time in a power outage. And if we drain the battery, we can always recharge it with the solar panel in the event of an extended power outage.

And that brings us to provisions.

The big thing here is just to keep an extra supply of all of the items we use on a daily basis: Contacts, saline, paper towels, toilet paper, soap, toothpaste, flashlights, batteries, first-aid kits… whatever else.

We can buy these things in bulk and replace them as we go. That way we always have plenty of everything on hand.

The easiest way to go about this is to take a month or two and document exactly what items we use and when we use them. From there we can determine what items we should keep extra quantities of on hand at all times.

Of course, this requires that we have some extra storage space available to us. I keep my back-up provisions on a few shelves in the basement. For those without a basement, perhaps a closet or shelves in the garage would work for storing provisions.

That's the basic idea behind home resiliency. Have a little back up energy and plenty of food, water, and stuff on hand… just in case.

Take note that none of this is about doomsday prepping. That's not what we're talking about here.

Home resiliency is simply about having the ability to be self-reliant for a reasonable period of time. To me, it's just a sensible thing to do.

That said, let's touch on some other alternative investments.

Personally, I love the idea of a personal wine cellar and a family garden. The return on investment with these probably isn't going to be monetary, but that doesn't mean there's not a return.

I also think it's worth looking into a whole-home generator and potentially an off-the-grid solar system. I love the idea of energy independence at the household level. And both of these items could provide that to a degree.

For whole-home generators, buying through Home Depot or Lowes is probably the easiest way to go. They both have zero-interest financing programs available as well.

Another interesting alternative investment is crowdlending. It's a quick and easy way to start generating passive income. Crowdlending revolves around platforms like Prosper. These platforms match borrowers up with lenders. Here's how it works…

Suppose somebody comes to Prosper and applies for a loan for credit consolidation or maybe a home improvement project. The platform does some basic due diligence on this person. It does a credit check and collects basic financial information. Then it scores the borrower based on their risk level and prices the loan accordingly. Riskier borrowers are assigned higher interest rates.

At that point, the platform puts the note out for crowd investments. Anyone who wants to lend the borrower a portion of their total loan can do so at the determined interest rate.

So let's say the borrower applied for a $20,000 loan. And let's imagine the crowdlending platform assigned the loan a 15.4 percent interest rate. Anyone who contributes to funding the loan will receive interest payments each month in proportion to how much they loaned.

In other words, crowdlending allows us to become the bank.

Now, I was very skeptical of this at first. I figured these platforms would only attract borrowers who could not secure financing from a traditional bank. As such, I expected the default rates to be high.

That isn't the case.

My experience has been that most borrowers pay on time each month. I've consistently generated returns between 9 percent and 15 percent by building a loan portfolio on Prosper.

Crowdlending is certainly worth exploring. We provide additional training on exactly how to build a robust crowdlending portfolio within our investment membership *The Phoenician League.*

Lastly, I'd like to put one final alternative investment on your radar. I highly recommend that everybody get up to speed on what are called security tokens.

Security tokens are a great combination of stocks and cryptocurrency. They convey ownership in the underlying asset like a stock. But they trade on a transparent platform like cryptocurrencies.

We're not just talking about optimizing investing here. Security tokens could create a market for assets that have never before been widely traded.

Think about all the collectibles that are out there right now. Artwork, classic cars, rare gold coins, baseball cards, old stamps, historical artifacts… the list could go on and on.

These collectibles all have value. But there isn't a liquid market for them today.

Security tokens will change that.

Security tokens will enable collectors to turn a fraction of whatever their collection is into a stock, and then it will trade on a security token exchange. What we're talking about here is a world in which we can own $1/100^{th}$ of a classic Ferrari. Or $1/1000^{th}$ of the Mona Lisa. Or $1/5^{th}$ of a classic 1907 St. Gauden gold coin.

There will be a liquid market where these assets constantly trade just like stocks and cryptocurrencies do today. We'll be able to buy and sell collectibles with ease.

And it won't just be collectibles.

Movies, television shows, songs and albums, and even commercial real estate will all be "tokenized" and trade as security tokens in the years to come. One day soon we'll be able to buy a small fraction of the Empire State Building or the Taj Mahal.

I find this to be a fascinating concept.

A company called T-Zero developed an exchange that can facilitate the trading of security tokens. The exchange has been up and running for years now with full regulatory approval, but there aren't many assets trading on it yet.

For anyone interested in security tokens, I would recommend setting up an account on T-Zero and learning the ropes.

It's a good idea to buy T-Zero's own digital asset TZROP on the exchange as well. It's basically a "picks and shovel" play on the whole space.

From there, we should keep an eye out for new listings on T-Zero. Right now there aren't many. But when we start to see more and more interesting offerings appear on T-Zero, that's when we know the security token boom is underway. When that happens I would expect TZROP to explode higher in price as well.

This concludes our discussion on asset allocation and alternative investments.

Next up we have to talk about the primary challenge we face from a macroeconomic standpoint today. Then we'll launch into how to implement a cash flow wealth strategy and become financially independent.

Key Points

- Asset allocation entails spreading our capital across several different asset classes
- Asset allocation provides true diversification… and ultimately financial security
- Asset allocation serves as the foundation that enables us to pursue a more focused wealth strategy
- How our investment membership can help
- The importance of alternative investments
- How to build true "home resiliency"
- The benefits of crowd-lending
- The appeal of security tokens

Action to take: If you would like to download our Asset Allocation Spreadsheet template, you can find it here: https://beyondthenestegg.com/extras/

And if you would like help with building a customized asset allocation model, give our investment membership *The Phoenician League* a look. You can get more information on our program right here: https://phoenicianleague.com/secret/

CHAPTER SEVEN

THE CHALLENGE WE FACE

People who are in or approaching retirement today face immense challenges that those who retired in the years before them did not. Why?

Simply put, we've been living in a bubble world since the 1980s, but the bubble popped in 2022.

I think most of us know this to be true. We can *feel* it. But this next chart tells the story quite well.[15]

[15] https://www.bloomberg.com/

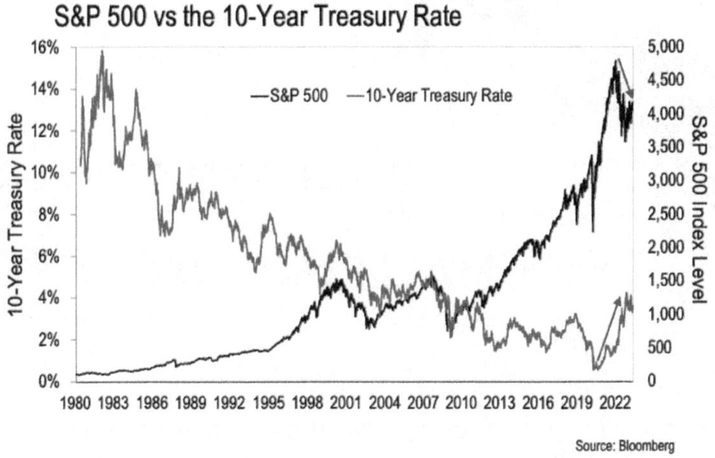

Here we can see the S&P 500 and the 10-year Treasury rate going back to 1980. The S&P 500 is the black line. And the 10-year Treasury rate is the blue line.

We're using the S&P 500 as a proxy for US stock prices. And we're using the 10-year Treasury as a proxy for interest rates. This chart makes it perfectly clear that the two are inversely correlated.

Interest rates started falling in 1982, and they fell consistently for the next 40 years. Meanwhile, US stocks consistently went up in value over that same time period.

But everything was reversed in 2022. Rates started going up, and stock prices started to fall. We can see those moves clearly marked by the red arrows on the chart above.

When we zoom out like this, it's no surprise that stocks fell hard when rates started to rise in 2022. But it sure caught a lot of people by surprise.

In fact, many financial analysts spent over 12 months trying to convince themselves and their clients that these moves were temporary. *Just wait for the Fed to pivot,* they said. *Then we'll get back to normal.*

But here's the thing—what happened from 1982 to 2022 was not normal. Nor was it organic.

Instead, it was all driven by the debasement of our money. The US government and the Federal Reserve (the Fed) worked hand-in-hand to create over $8 trillion dollars from thin air during this time period.

We can see this very clearly simply by looking at what happened to the Fed's balance sheet.

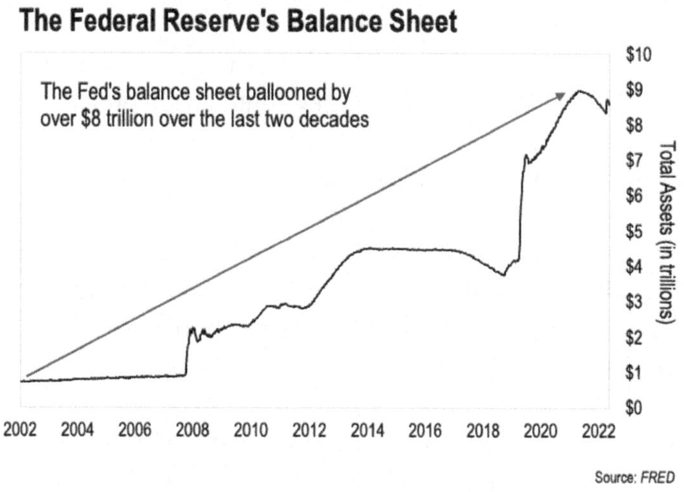

Here we can see that the Fed's balance sheet grew by over $8 trillion from 2002 to 2022.[16]

[16] https://fred.stlouisfed.org/series/WALCL

The key here is that when we see this line going up, that's the Fed creating new dollars from thin air. The Fed used those new dollars to buy financial assets—US Treasury bonds and mortgage-backed securities. That's why its balance sheet ballooned.

These new dollars are what drove interest rates down to nearly zero. They are also what bid US stock prices up tremendously. Essentially, the funny money decoupled interest rates and stock prices from the underlying economy.

In other words, these trillions of dollars created from nothing "financialized" everything. They turned the stock market into a giant casino. Except the game was rigged such that stock prices only went up over time.

Thus, this time period—1982 to 2022—will go down in history as *The Age of Paper Wealth*. It was a time when people truly believed that printing money could create prosperity.

Of course, it was all an illusion.

The problem is, nobody born after 1960 has known anything else in their adult life. All we've ever known is falling interest rates and rising stock prices. Our approach to personal finance reflects this.

Everybody has been encouraged to plan for retirement by pouring their savings into financial assets—stocks and various kinds of funds.

That approach made some sense in a world where rates only go down and stocks only go up. But if we've left that world—

if the Age of Paper Wealth has ended—does it still make sense to manage our finances this way?

I don't think so. It's time to rethink personal finance 101.

And that brings us to our second major challenge...

The term "inflation" is thrown around quite a bit today. If you ask somebody what it means, they will tell you rising prices. But if you ask them what causes inflation, most people can't give you a meaningful answer. So let's demystify inflation for a minute.

First of all, I am sympathetic to the definition put forth by the Austrian School of Economics. Inflation is the expansion of the money supply. It is the act of creating new money and injecting it into the economy.[17]

If we speak from a dollar-centric point of view, inflation occurs when the Fed and the US Treasury pump new dollars into the system. These dollars then have to go somewhere. Wherever they go, we are likely to see rising prices follow.

From this perspective, rising prices are the result of inflation. They are not inflation itself. And prices do not rise in a uniform manner.

Let's zoom in on two situations to illustrate this concept.

First, we'll look at the 2008 financial crisis. Then we'll look at the COVID-19 event.

---

[17] https://mises.org/library/defining-inflation

The Fed pumped over $3.6 trillion into the financial system in response to the 2008 financial crisis.[18] Again we're talking about new dollars created from nothing.

Here's the chart:

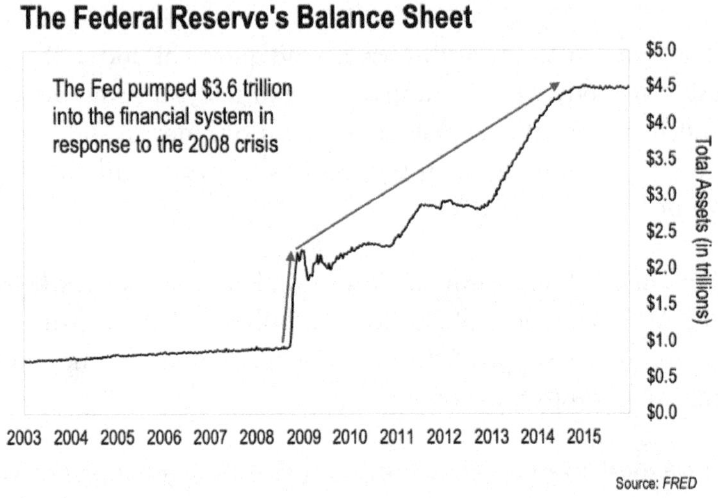

Source: FRED

This is a chart of the assets on the Fed's balance sheet. These consist mostly of US Treasury bonds, though the Fed bought a bunch of mortgage-backed securities in the wake of the 2008 crisis as well.

Remember, when the line goes up, that's the Fed creating new money from nothing, to buy assets.

[18] https://fred.stlouisfed.org/series/WALCL

Let's use August 2008 as our starting point here. At that time the Fed held $898 billion in assets on its balance sheet. Fast forward to January 2015, and that number hit $4.5 trillion.

So, the Fed created roughly $3.6 trillion from thin air to buy US Treasuries and mortgage-backed securities in response to the 2008 crisis. When those transactions settled, the new money was injected into the system.

This was absolutely considered an extreme response. The Fed had never initiated such aggressive asset purchase programs before.

However, we didn't see prices for consumer goods rise tremendously in response to the Fed's actions. Instead, most of the inflation flowed into the stock market. This set off an epic boom that lasted over a decade.

From the Fed's perspective, this was a fantastic result. Nobody ever complains about their stock portfolio going up.

And the Fed even made an effort to gradually taper its balance sheet after the dust settled. It gradually reduced its assets from $4.5 trillion in 2015 to $4.1 trillion by 2020.

Then came the COVID-19 event. And the Fed followed the exact same "crisis response" game plan.

Here's the chart:

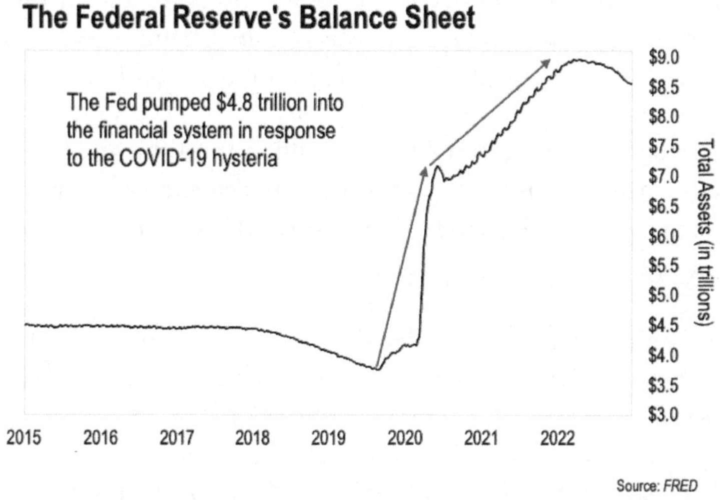

As we can see, the Fed pumped roughly $4.8 trillion into the financial system in response to COVID-19. This expanded its balance sheet from about $4.1 trillion in February 2020 to nearly $9 trillion by February 2022.[19]

What's more, the US Treasury directly injected more than $5 trillion into the economy via various COVID-19 "stimulus" plans as well. That's in addition to the money that the Fed pumped into the financial system.

Perhaps it's no surprise then that the results were dramatically different this time.

Now, the Fed's chosen metric to measure inflation is the Consumer Price Index (CPI). And in January 2022 the CPI hit its highest level in 40 years. This seemed to shock mainstream financial pundits.

---

[19] https://fred.stlouisfed.org/series/WALCL

And here's the thing—the CPI is a lowball number. It understates how fast consumer prices are rising.

That's because the CPI employs a replacement cost model. When the price of a particular good rises too much, the model takes it out and swaps in a comparable lower-cost good. This assumes that consumers will adjust to rising prices by changing their spending habits.

For example, if the price of steak goes up too much, the CPI may swap it out for ground beef. The idea is that consumers will buy more ground beef and less steak in this scenario.

But that doesn't change the fact that steak prices went up. The CPI ignores this by dropping it from the model. And that's the whole point. The CPI always understates inflation.

That's why assets with inflation protection mechanisms tied to the CPI such as Treasury Inflation-Protected Securities (TIPS) just aren't adequate. It's also why Social Security's cost of living adjustment never seems to keep up with costs of living.

The key point here is that consumer price inflation is baked into the cake for as long as the Fed and the Treasury can create dollars from nothing.

This virtually guarantees that national "retirement" plans like Social Security are doomed. These plans will continue to send out checks to people for years to come, but thanks to inflation those checks just won't buy much. Any financial strategy that doesn't account for these challenges is also doomed.

The good news is that there's a solution to these financial pitfalls. In fact, financial independence is more achievable today than ever before. It just requires a deeper understanding of the financial system. This is something that we won't find in any textbook.

To me, the answer starts with asset allocation—as we have already discussed. But that's just the starting point.

Asset allocation provides us with a fundamental "base" of operations. But to become financially independent we must use that base as a jump-off point. We must create a comprehensive wealth strategy focused on building multiple streams of income. This includes utilizing complex legal entities and arcane sections of the tax code.

What we're talking about here is drastically different from the traditional financial plan. To illustrate this, let's talk again about what's sold as the "normal" financial plan. It's all about retirement.

Retirement is sold as this magical period where we don't have to work anymore. Suddenly we will be free to do whatever we want to do, whenever we want to do it.

And I know for some retirees, that is their experience. But I also know that many others are miserable. They sit around watching TV all day because they don't have anything better to do. There's no meaning there.

That's at least partly because of how we are told to plan for retirement.

The conventional wisdom tells us to save a small portion of our income throughout our working years and lock it away in "qualified" retirement plans. For wage earners, these are 401(k)s and IRAs.

The idea is that we need to get to a certain "number" that we can live on in retirement.

Maybe it's $1 million… Maybe it's $3 million… Whatever it is, the thinking is flawed for a few reasons.

First off, the "number" we reach isn't our actual number. At least not with 401(k)s and IRAs. Instead, we will be required to pay ordinary income taxes on every withdrawal we ever make from those accounts.

Now, if our only source of income in retirement is Social Security then this may not be a big deal. We won't have much income coming in, so our tax bill will be small, but that means we would have to live very frugally for the rest of our lives. That's probably not the kind of retirement most people envision.

On the other hand, if we do have other income sources in retirement, our ordinary tax rate could be 20 percent, 30 percent, or even higher. That means our tax bill would be substantial.

That brings us to another major fallacy with this kind of retirement planning. The whole idea that we spend our lives working to accumulate capital, only to consume that capital over our lifetimes is both foolish and destructive. That's my view.

Instead, the capital we accumulate should work for us. It should throw off income for us so we never have to deplete it. We can live on the income and keep the principal intact.

That's where our wealth strategy comes in. It shouldn't focus on trying to get to a number. Instead, it should focus on increasing our income and generating monthly cash flow. Cash flow is king.

As for the specifics, I happen to believe that rental real estate is the way to go.

In fact, my experience is that it's not terribly difficult to go from zero to $10,000 per month in passive income with real estate. Some people can get there in six years or less. For others it may take 10–12 years.

But that's only if they do it right. And doing it right requires a comprehensive approach. This includes fundamental analysis, deal flow, advanced tax strategies, and sound asset protection structure.

We're going to talk about all of these items in the coming chapters. But first, I think it's critical we understand the nuances of the systems within which we live. We'll do so in the next chapter.

Key Points

- We've been living in a bubble world since the 1980s, but the bubble popped in 2022
- This is illustrated by the long-term correlation between equity prices and interest rates

- Interest rates fell consistently from 1982 through 2022
- Equity prices rose consistently from 1982 through 2022
- These long-term trends were driven by the debasement of money—we see this clearly when we analyze the Fed's balance sheet
- Printing trillions of dollars from nothing decoupled interest rates and stock prices from the underlying economy—this is the "financialization" of everything
- The period from 1982 to 2022 will go down in history as *The Age of Paper Wealth*
- That age is over, thus, we need to rethink personal finance 101
- Inflation is baked into the current monetary system
- The CPI always understates inflation
- Any financial strategy that doesn't account for inflation is doomed
- The good news is, financial independence is more attainable today than ever before… we just have to adjust our approach

CHAPTER EIGHT

WISDOM AND UNDERSTANDING

There's no wisdom without understanding.

This statement explains why so many people struggle today. And that struggle isn't simply financial. It's mental. And it's spiritual as well.

The lack of understanding breeds worry. And one simply cannot be content or confident with worries on the mind. I've heard it said that people at the turn of the 20th century did not have this problem. That's because life was simpler back then.

People had central heating, refrigeration, and access to abundant food at their local markets. They had what they considered rapid rail transportation, basic medical care, and long-distance communication in the form of telegrams and radios.

And they had optimism.

Cars, televisions, electricity, telephones, and even airplanes were quickly becoming a reality. Positive change was taking place right before their eyes.

These items allowed relatively comfortable living arrangements for many people in the developed world. Certainly more comfortable than any generation that had come before. At least that we know of.

But it's what they didn't have that made all the difference. It's what they didn't have that made their world *understandable*.

To start with, there were no income taxes in America at the turn of the 20th century. Whatever you earned, you kept. This placed far more purchasing power in the hands of everybody.

As a direct result, there wasn't a massive and complex tax code to deal with. In fact, there was no tax code at all. The IRS didn't exist. As such, Americans didn't have to file a tax return year after year.

In addition, there were no excessive regulations. This enabled anyone to start a small business with ease. And it allowed people to transact with one another as they saw fit without any arbitrary rules or red tape.

This also provided for a simple and understandable legal code. Don't hurt people and don't take their stuff. Simple, easy to remember.

Of course, that means there weren't legions of lawyers running around chasing ambulances and looking for frivolous lawsuits like they do today. This is an incredibly unproductive activity that wastes time and resources.

At the turn of the 20 century, Americans still had sound money. That is to say, they had money that couldn't be created from nothing—because it was backed by gold. Thus, they did not have to contend with inflation and dollars that constantly lose purchasing power as we do today.

They also did not have countless media sources vying for their attention every second of every day. No television ads. No social media. No phone calls or text messages. They could more easily keep their mind focused on that which was most important to them. And I suspect their personal relationships were much richer as a result.

Perhaps more importantly, they didn't have someone trying to convince them that the sky was falling all the time. That's exactly what the news does to us today.

And the technological advances of the day were also understandable. Those I mentioned—cars, televisions, electricity, telephones, airplanes—are each easy to understand. Even if we don't know how they work, we can see and comprehend what they do.

For comparison, try to explain artificial intelligence (AI), machine learning, deep neural networks, brain-computer interfaces, quantum computing, nanotechnology, and all the other technological developments in the works today.

Not only do we not understand these things—at least most of us don't—we also don't know exactly what these things do. Or how they will impact us in the future. We can't "see" them in action.

Putting it all together, the guy living in the early 1900s could go to work, save a lot of money in a short period of time, buy a house, raise a family, and pursue his interests with relative ease and confidence—all with just an average salary.

That's not conjecture, either. It was not uncommon for the average home to cost about twice the median salary in the US at the time.

Last I checked, the median salary in the US today is about $69,000 per year.[20] If the common home cost about twice the median salary, we should expect to see the average home price at around $138,000.

Not a chance, right? Today, the average home often costs between three and a half and five times the median salary. What this means is people could once buy their home without going deep into debt and without having to put up a big mortgage payment every month.

And absent inflation, they could build capital simply by saving money in the bank or even under the mattress. They didn't have to take risks with their savings. And they certainly didn't have to set up complex legal structures to protect their assets. By the way, we'll talk about how to do this later in the book.

But here's the point…

Our civilization has become massively complex over the last one hundred years. The rules of the game changed. Today, simply working hard and saving money isn't a winning strategy. You don't get ahead that way. Not if that's all you do.

---

[20] https://www.census.gov/quickfacts/fact/table/US/PST045222

The good news is that our world is not too difficult to understand, if we change our lens. This just requires us to change the way we think about some core aspects of our civilization as it exists today.

Specifically, we need to change the way we think about government, money, and taxes. That's what this chapter is all about. As I mentioned before, these ideas might not be comfortable—at least not at first. They certainly aren't taught in schools or textbooks.

But it's critical we understand these key institutions, as they exist today. I think this is a prerequisite if we want to build a sustainable plan for financial independence.

With understanding, comes wisdom. With wisdom, comes confidence.

Understanding Government

We will focus on the US federal government here, but what we discuss applies to nearly all governments in the developed world as well.

And we have to start with this—the government is not what our Social Studies textbooks say it is.

It is not the wise arbiter of disputes. It is not the mighty protector of the people. It is not the great sage that solves all the world's problems. And it is certainly not the endless cornucopia of abundance that can provide everything to everybody… if we would only allow it to do so.

Government is force. It is the entity that claims a monopoly on violence within a specific geographic area. That makes it dangerous.

The American founders were aware of this. Here's George Washington:[21]

> *Government is not reason. It is not eloquence. It is force. Like fire it is a dangerous servant and a fearful master. Never for a moment should it be left to irresponsible action.*

Here's Thomas Jefferson:[22]

> *That government is best which governs the least.*

And here's Thomas Paine:[23]

> *Government, even in its best state, is but a necessary evil. In its worst state, an intolerable one.*

---

21 https://www.mountvernon.org/library/digitalhistory/digital-encyclopedia/article/spurious-quotations/

22 https://www.monticello.org/research-education/thomas-jefferson-encyclopedia/government-best-which-governs-least-spurious-quotation/

23 https://fee.org/articles/thomas-paine-on-government-liberty-and-power/

This apprehensive view of government persisted in America for about 140 years after its founding, give or take a decade. That's why private associations and mutual aid societies were so prominent back then. Americans knew that whatever civil functions needed to be done, it was people in the local community, not the government, that were responsible for them.

French political scientist Alexis de Tocqueville expressed this dynamic best upon his visit to the US in the 1830s. He wrote:[24]

> *Americans of all ages, all conditions, and all dispositions constantly form associations... The Americans make associations to give entertainment, to found seminaries, to build inns, to construct churches, to diffuse books... Wherever at the end of some new undertaking you see the government in France, or a man of rank in England, in the United States you will be sure to find an association.*

This quote speaks to the principles of mutual collaboration and personal responsibility. That's what self-sustaining communities require.

Now, you might wonder what any of this has to do with personal finance...

And the answer is: *everything.*

[24] https://press.uchicago.edu/Misc/Chicago/805328.html

We live in a world today in which the government makes the rules, and it can then change them at any time, for any reason. That's regardless of how much hardship it might cause us.

It's important for us to understand this dynamic. We should not assume that the government is on our side, even if we do everything the right way.

When you get into real estate—where you invest makes all the difference.

As investors in certain states found out back in 2020, some state governments are openly hostile to real estate investors. A few even encouraged tenants to stop paying rent. Then they made it impossible for the property owners to evict tenants for breach of contract.

In other words, the government is all too happy to violate centuries of established contract law when they see it as in their interests to do so. This is a direct threat to financial independence. We need to be aware of that.

Of course, good men and women have been rushing off to the voting booth for decades now in an effort to vote for the politicians who will usher in their vision for a "better" government. It just never seems to work. So people go rushing out to the voting booth once again when the next election comes, certain that *this time* they can affect lasting change.

It never comes. And that's because the government is not what most people think it is.

The main point I want to emphasize here is that we need to keep our focus on what's practical.

Modern government has erected massively complex tax and legal codes. While these things are arcane, there is a method to the madness.

The common belief is that the tax code is all about raising revenue for the government to fund civil services. In just the same way, we tend to think that the legal code is about preventing crime and reprimanding criminals.

But this is wrong on both counts. Let's start with taxes.

The tax code is *actually* about how not to pay taxes. It was written to show us how to legally avoid paying taxes.

Think about this—the federal tax code consists of over 70,000 pages. Yet, less than 5 percent of those pages are about paying taxes. In other words, less than 5 percent of the tax code pertains to collecting revenue for the government.

The other 95 percent is all about how to avoid paying the taxes that the first 5 percent says we owe. That's the whole point underlying such a complex code.

Upon hearing this, many people may want to cry foul. *That's not fair*, they might say.

To the contrary, it is fair. It is 100 percent fair. And here's why—the tax code applies the same to everybody. Nobody gets special treatment. If you understand and follow the tax code, you can reduce your taxes.

It doesn't matter if you are rich or poor… black or white… Christian, Muslim, or atheist… none of it. Anyone who follows the tax code can pay less in taxes.

You see what I'm saying here?

Now I'm not saying that we should favor the tax code as it is. It makes life incredibly complex for those who follow it, and it makes life incredibly difficult for those who don't. But it applies to everyone equally. In that way it is fair.

Here's the thing—the tax code is simply a set of financial incentives. The government decides what it wants people to do with their money and then builds tax breaks around those activities.

These are things like investing in affordable housing, private early-stage companies, energy production, economic development zones, conservation easements, and others. These actions have been incentivized in the tax code for decades.

That said, the incentives are prone to change from time to time.

For example, the tax code has incentivized investing in oil and gas for decades now. But the political winds shifted more toward incentivizing investment in renewable energy in recent years.

And that's the key… new incentives always replace old incentives. That's the nature of modern government.

The people who take advantage of these incentives to lower their taxes have a far easier time becoming financially independent. After all, it's darn near impossible to get there if one-third to one-half of our income is confiscated from us through taxation every year.

The legal code follows the same dynamic. It's complicated, but it's really just an incentive system.

Delaware corporations, Wyoming LLCs, living trusts, shell companies—successful investors and businessmen create a complex web of legal entities specifically to shield their money from taxes and their assets from lawsuits.

Like it or not, it's all a game. And it's not a terribly difficult game to play once we understand the rules.

I'm amazed that most people today spend 12 to 16 years of their life in school, and yet they learn absolutely nothing about how the real world works when it comes to money, finance, taxes, and legal entities. That makes no sense. And it's why so many people struggle today.

But the good news is that we can employ CPAs and attorneys to help us with this stuff. These are the professionals who can help set us up for financial independence. Our tax strategy and our wealth strategy need to work hand-in-hand.

I would like it to be different. Things were simpler at the turn of the 20th century and human civilization got along just fine. Perhaps better in many ways. I suspect people were happier.

But we cannot go back to how things were. Time is like a river. It only flows in one direction.

So eventually the structure of our civilization today will change. But until it does, we have to play by the rules as they currently exist.

That's why it is critical we understand the nature of modern government and what it is doing with its tax and legal codes.

With understanding, comes wisdom. With wisdom, comes confidence.

Key Points

- There's no wisdom without understanding
- The world was easier to understand at the turn of the 20th century
- Our civilization has become far more complex over the last 120 years
- Working hard and saving money is no longer a winning strategy today
- To get ahead today, we must change the way we think about government, money, and taxes
- The government makes the rules… and it can change them at any time
- The US tax code is not about collecting revenue for the government—it's about how to legally avoid paying taxes
- The tax code is fair—it applies the same to everybody
- Our tax strategy and our wealth strategy need to work hand-in-hand
- With understanding comes wisdom; with wisdom comes confidence

CHAPTER NINE

THE FAST TRACK TO FINANCIAL INDEPENDENCE

Now it's time to talk about wealth strategy.

Everything up to this point has been about knowledge, understanding, and building a strong asset base. All that is critical for building our foundation. Once the foundation is in place, we have to use it as a jump-off point. And it all starts with mindset.

When we talk about wealth strategy, we are talking about an intensely focused approach to building wealth.

Think about horse racing here. When people race horses, they put blinders on them. The blinders restrict their field of vision so that they can only see what's in front of them.

Do you know why they do that? Because if the horse has full range of vision, it might start paying attention to what the horse in the next lane is doing. And if it does that, the risk that it will drift out of its own lane and wipe out goes up significantly.

I think about wealth strategy in just the same way. It's about focusing exclusively on the finish line every second, every step.

And that leads us to the big question—what's our finish line? What are we shooting for?

For me, it was always financial independence. I don't want to be stuck working a job for the rest of my life. I don't want to be on somebody else's timeline forever.

Instead, I want to build a portfolio of assets that will produce income for me, month in and month out. And I'm going to keep doing this until that income is enough to cover all my expenses. Then I can spend my time doing things that truly matter to me.

The late Gary North used to talk about the difference between a job and a calling.

Your job puts food on the table and pays the bills. Your calling is that one productive thing in life that you can do better than everybody else. Or at least almost everybody else.

To me, building wealth is all about creating the ability to pursue my calling.

I couldn't care less about cars, status, entertainment, luxury items, or anything of the sort. Those things are hollow. They don't provide meaning.

What I care about is living a purpose-driven life. I want to be a good steward of the blessings I have received, and I want to use those blessings to have a positive impact on my tiny little corner of the world.

It's this driving thought that enabled me to focus intensely on my wealth strategy. I don't think chasing material goods would have been the same motivator.

My point is this—if you want to become financially independent, it requires focus and commitment. And of course, it requires a strong strategy.

I believe that this strategy needs to focus on cash flow. Anybody who has experienced material paper losses in a market downturn will understand why immediately.

This is very different from the asset allocation strategy that we discussed earlier.

Asset allocation is about building a diversified asset portfolio. That's all about resiliency. If we run into an emergency, we have assets to fall back on. And that's critical. We have to start there.

But that approach only goes so far. If we continue to diversify across different assets after we've built the foundation, it's going to take us a long time to become financially independent.

As we've discussed, traditional financial planning focuses on capital gains. It's all about building a "nest egg" by investing in things like stocks, bonds, and index funds.

The idea is that if you can build your nest egg to a big enough number, you'll have enough money to retire. Typically we expect to take 30 or 40 years to get to that point.

But if we think about it, the whole point of doing this is so that we can retire and live off the money we accumulated. Basically, we convert our nest egg to income in retirement.

So that begs the question… why not just focus on building income in the first place? If that's the end goal, why take the long, roundabout way to get there?

Simply put, we shouldn't.

I can say from first-hand experience that it's not very difficult to create an extra $3,000–$5,000 in passive income every month. Anyone with a decent salary can do this in three or four years if they are focused.

And ultimately I think it's possible for most people to create an extra $10,000 per month in passive income in six to twelve years. That of course depends on their current situation and level of commitment. But it's 100 percent doable.

I bet most of us could live comfortably on $10,000 a month. So then, how do we get there?

My answer is rental real estate. Let's talk about why…

Cash Flow is King

Cash flow is king. Period.

That's my real estate investment philosophy, and there is no compromising it.

I know there are people out there who love to talk about the hottest up-and-coming markets where prices are about to blow up. I have no interest in that game. In fact, I think that mindset—the idea that real estate investing is about finding a hot market—is bound to get many investors in deep trouble.

There's a very simple trade-off in real estate when it comes to analyzing markets and properties. When the market is hot, the cash flow is typically low.

Cash flow is simply the monthly rental income we receive minus the monthly mortgage payment, property taxes, homeowners insurance, management fees, and any homeowners association (HOA) dues.

In other words, cash flow is what's left over after we use a property's rent to pay all its expenses. And the beautiful thing about this is that we know what our cash flow will be for any property we're analyzing *before* we buy it.

If we stop to think about it—that dynamic is amazing.

With real estate, there's no guessing what our return on investment (ROI) will be. That's because the ROI for any property depends upon its monthly rent, purchase price, insurance costs, property taxes, management fees, and HOA dues (if any).

We know each of these numbers up front. So when we run the numbers and find that a property wouldn't produce adequate cash flow for us, we don't buy it. Simple.

Imagine if investing in the stock market were like this.

As we know, a stock's ROI depends largely on capital appreciation. That means for us to get a return, the stock has to go up.

So if investing in the stock market were like investing in real estate, we would be able to know if a stock was going to go up and by how much, ahead of time. And if the stock wasn't going to go up, we wouldn't buy it.

Of course, that's not how it works. Nobody truly knows if a stock is going to go up. So we don't know what our rate of return will be.

The beautiful thing about investing in real estate for cash flow is that we do in fact know what our return will be. Now, we don't know if our property will go up in value or not. But we don't care. We're in it for the monthly cash flow.

Of course that begs the question—how do you know what "good" cash flow is?

All we have to do is measure the ROI by assessing two things—the cash-on-cash return and the return on equity.

To illustrate, let's look at an example.

Purchase Price:	$128,000		
Down Payment:	$32,000	Valuation:	$128,000
Interest Rate:	5.500%	Mortgage:	$96,000
Rent:	$1,150	Equity:	**$32,000**
Mortgage:	$662	80% LTV:	$102,400
Management:	$115	Equity Available:	$6,400
Cash Flow:	**$373**	Return on Equity:	14.0%
Annual Cash Flow:	$4,473		
Cash on Cash Return:	14.0%		

I pulled this directly from my rental real estate spreadsheet. This is a potential investment that I considered as I was writing this book.

Let's focus on the left side of this graphic first.

As we can see this is a single family home with a purchase price of $128,000. The minimum required down payment is 20 percent, but lenders often offer a slightly better rate when we put 25 percent down on a property. So that's what's reflected here. 25 percent of $128,000 is $32,000.

At the time that I was considering this property I could lock in a rate of 5.5 percent. And my property manager in the area confirmed they could rent out the property for $1,150 a month.

To determine if this is a good investment, all we have to do is run the numbers.

First, if we're paying $32,000 down on this property, that means our mortgage will be $96,000.

If we go to an online mortgage calculator—I use www.mortgagecalculator.org—we'll find that the principal plus interest payment on a $96,000 mortgage at 5.5 percent is $545. Then if we escrow property taxes and homeowners insurance, the total mortgage payment comes out to $662 a month.

Now we have to add in property management fees to calculate the property's total monthly expenses. This is what we pay the property management company to find a tenant, collect monthly rent, and handle any maintenance items that pop up.

Generally property management fees will be 8–10 percent of the property's gross monthly rent. That just depends on the market. In this case they are 10 percent. That equates to $115 a month.

So we add our property management costs to our mortgage payment to get our total expenses for this property. In this case that's $777 a month.

Since we can get $1,150 a month in rent, our monthly cash flow would be $373 a month. That's just $1,150 minus $777.

Now the question is—is this good?

To answer that, we have to run the numbers to get our cash on cash return. This figure tells us what our ROI would be relative to how much money it costs us to buy the property. To calculate the cash-on-cash return, we simply annualize the monthly cash flow and divide it into our down payment.

To annualize our monthly cash flow, we multiply it by twelve. So $373 a month times twelve months gives us $4,473. That's how much income this property will produce each year.

Then if we take $4,473 and divide it by our $32,000 down payment, that gives us a cash-on-cash return of 14 percent.

So now we have to ask—is a 14 percent return on our money good?

To answer this, we need to compare this return to the return we could get on other investments.

As I write, ten-year US Treasury bonds are paying about 3.4 percent per year. And most bank certificates of deposit (CDs) are still paying well under 1.5 percent per year.

In comparison to those investments, yes, this is a fantastic deal.

What about compared to the stock market?

Historically, a 10 percent annual return has been considered great for stocks. Sure, some years the market vastly outperforms this number. But other years stocks produce a negative return. Plus, the average investor tends to underperform the market consistently.

Not to mention, the cash-on-cash return is just one way we make money with real estate. It doesn't include our equity build-up, tax benefits, and capital appreciation.

So personally, I consider 14 percent to be an excellent cash-on-cash return for any property that's rent-ready. That said, we still need to compare this to other investment properties available.

For example, let's compare this to a second rental property that I also considered as I was writing this book.

Here are the numbers for the property we just analyzed:

Purchase Price:	$128,000		
Down Payment:	$32,000	Valuation:	$128,000
Interest Rate:	5.500%	Mortgage:	$96,000
Rent:	$1,150	Equity:	**$32,000**
Mortgage:	$662	80% LTV:	$102,400
Management:	$115	Equity Available:	$6,400
Cash Flow:	**$373**	Return on Equity:	14.0%
Annual Cash Flow:	$4,473		
Cash on Cash Return:	14.0%		

And here are the numbers for an alternative property:

Purchase Price:	$325,000		
Down Payment:	$81,250	Valuation:	$325,000
Interest Rate:	5.500%	Mortgage:	$243,750
Rent:	$2,300	Equity:	**$81,250**
Mortgage:	$1,748	80% LTV:	$260,000
Management:	$0	Equity Available:	$16,250
Cash Flow:	**$552**	Return on Equity:	8.2%
Annual Cash Flow:	$6,624		
Cash on Cash Return:	8.2%		

As we can see, this property costs more to buy, yet it produces more monthly cash flow—$552 a month compared to $373 a month.

If we were to simply compare these two properties based on cash flow, we would have to say $552 a month is better than $373 a month, right?

One would think! But look at our cash-on-cash return figures. The first property can produce a return of 14 percent. This second property only delivers a cash-on-cash return of 8.2 percent. This tells us that we can get more "bang for our buck" with the first property. We get a proportionately higher cash flow for less money down.

Given these two options, we should invest in the first property, right?

Well, it depends.

This first property is a home in Birmingham, AL, that was built in 1950. It's located in an urban neighborhood. It has three bedrooms, two bathrooms, and no garage.

Meanwhile, the second property is a newer home in a suburb outside of Oklahoma City, OK. It was built in 2022. It has four bedrooms, two bathrooms, and a two-car garage.

Obviously with newer properties, we shouldn't have to worry about any big repairs for at least four or five years—maybe more. On the other hand, a lot more could go wrong with homes that are now over 70 years old.

So the first option is "riskier" than the second. We would almost certainly have more repairs to deal with. And of course that's something we have to pay for as real estate investors. Any big repairs would reduce our return on investment.

We also need to consider each market. Birmingham and Oklahoma City are very different.

Fortunately both markets are in very business-friendly, landlord-friendly states. As I write this book, however, Oklahoma City is experiencing a lot more growth.

Plus, the larger, new construction home caters to a different kind of tenant than the smaller home built in the 1950s. That's neither good nor bad, but it's something to be aware of.

So given these two options, which one do we pick?

It all depends on our personal investment criteria. And that's going to be the subject of our next chapter.

Key Points

- Our wealth strategy is an intensely focused approach to building wealth
- It's all about financial independence—building income streams that exceed our expenses
- Financial independence enables us to pursue our true calling
- It's possible to create $3,000—$5,000 in extra income with real estate in three or four years if we're focused
- From there, getting to $10,000 a month in extra income is possible in six to twelve years
- When investing in real estate, we should focus on monthly cash flow—not price appreciation
- If we focus on cash flow, we know what our ROI will be right up front
- We assess ROI with two metrics: cash-on-cash return and return on equity

Action to take: Would you like a clean template for analyzing the numbers regarding real estate investments? We've made our analysis spreadsheet available to you at: https://beyondthenestegg.com/extras/

CHAPTER TEN

GETTING STARTED WITH REAL ESTATE

Now it's time to talk about establishing real estate investment criteria. This is absolutely critical.

We saw in our example last chapter that the cash-on-cash return for any given property doesn't tell the full story. We also need to differentiate between newer properties and older properties, as well as their specific characteristics.

What we're talking about here is the difference between experts and amateur investors. Here's why…

When amateur investors come across a new investment opportunity, they analyze it… and then they make an investment decision based on their analysis. This requires them to make a new decision on each and every investment they consider.

Expert investors do the opposite.

Experts make their investment decisions *first*. That becomes their criteria. Then they look for opportunities that match up with their criteria.

Expert investors must still analyze every new opportunity, but they are grounded by their criteria. That provides context. If a property fits their criteria, they pull the trigger. If it doesn't, they pass.

In this way, expert investors don't have to make a new decision every time they assess a property. They already made their decision to buy or walk away when they established their criteria. This takes all the guesswork out of the analysis. And it eliminates the possibility for impulse purchases based on "what ifs."

At some point, we will inevitably come across absolutely beautiful properties in terrific locations from time to time. Everything may be perfect—except the cash-on-cash return is a little low. That little voice in our head may say, "What if I buy this property and it doubles in price? If that happens, it won't matter that the rate of return is lower than my criteria…"

We are all prone to that type of rationalization, right?

But if we give in to the "what ifs," we become like a rudderless ship at sea. We can be easily blown about with the changing winds.

That's why it's so critical to establish our investment criteria up front. Our criteria is our anchor. And it eradicates these what if scenarios entirely. Our criteria ensures that we aren't tempted to stray from our path.

Being firm on our criteria also helps us compare two opportunities that each look good, but in different ways. To illustrate this, let's go back to our examples from the previous chapter.

Property One

Purchase Price:	$128,000		
Down Payment:	$32,000	Valuation:	$128,000
Interest Rate:	5.500%	Mortgage:	$96,000
Rent:	$1,150	Equity:	**$32,000**
Mortgage:	$662	80% LTV:	$102,400
Management:	$115	Equity Available:	$6,400
Cash Flow:	**$373**	Return on Equity:	14.0%
Annual Cash Flow:	$4,473		
Cash on Cash Return:	14.0%		

Property Two

Purchase Price:	$325,000		
Down Payment:	$81,250	Valuation:	$325,000
Interest Rate:	5.500%	Mortgage:	$243,750
Rent:	$2,300	Equity:	**$81,250**
Mortgage:	$1,748	80% LTV:	$260,000
Management:	$0	Equity Available:	$16,250
Cash Flow:	**$552**	Return on Equity:	8.2%
Annual Cash Flow:	$6,624		
Cash on Cash Return:	8.2%		

Remember these?

The first property was built in 1950. It's located in an urban neighborhood in Birmingham, AL. The second property was built in 2022. And it's in a suburb outside of Oklahoma City, OK.

We can see that our cash-on-cash return is better for the Birmingham property. But as we discussed, this property is also riskier.

Obviously, we would almost certainly have far fewer repairs pop-up with the newer home in Oklahoma City. Meanwhile, there are plenty of little things that can go wrong with older homes.

As real estate investors, we have to fix everything that goes wrong. That costs money, which reduces our rate of return.

So there's a risk/reward element at play here. And that means we need to be solid on our investment criteria to choose between these two properties.

Generally speaking, investors who could not afford to cover out-of-pocket repairs costing five to ten thousand dollars should likely choose the newer property in this example. They will have years to build up a reserve using the property's cash flow before any big repairs are likely to hit.

But for those investors who would be comfortable handling a repair costing $5,000 to $10,000 out of their own pocket, the Birmingham property might make more sense. It cash flows better, and we might even buy two or three similar properties with the same funds we would have to put down on the one Oklahoma property.

So this brings us to what our investment criteria should contain.

For rental real estate, our criteria should clearly state the following items:

- The types of properties we want to buy
- Our minimum acceptable cash-on-cash return
- Our desired allocation of newer versus older properties
- The markets in which we would like to invest

For example, when I first got started in real estate, my criteria was to buy new construction single family homes in Dallas generating at least a 10 percent cash-on-cash return. I wanted "low risk" properties that would let me get in and learn the game. And I didn't want to worry about any surprise repairs while I was learning the ropes.

At the same time, I didn't want to chase anything under a 10 percent cash-on-cash return. At the time, I didn't need to because interest rates were well below 5 percent. I've since reduced my cash-on-cash return expectations to 7 percent for new construction properties.

I also established in my criteria that I wanted to build my portfolio by acquiring three new construction properties before adding an older home. And that's exactly what I did.

The benefit of going heavy on newer properties first is that we can build up a suitable cash reserve for each property without having to worry about repairs.

So I started with three new construction properties and I let each of them build up six months' worth of cash reserves. Only then did I take on my first older property.

My criteria was to only consider older properties that were capable of producing cash-on-cash returns above 13 percent. When I found one that met my criteria, I pulled the trigger.

I saw this as a way to add a little juice to my portfolio once I could afford to handle any repairs that might pop up.

My first older property performed so well that I decided to buy two more older properties before getting back to new construction. Once I had plenty of cash reserves in place, I decided that I was comfortable with a one-for-one allocation between new construction and older homes.

I share this with you only to point out that our investment criteria will likely evolve over time. But it's advisable to start with ultra-specific, conservative criteria until we have some experience under our belt.

Alright, before we move on I want to address a burning question new investors often have…

Do you have to start with single-family homes? What about multi-family properties? Which is better?

The answer is that you can start wherever you want, as long as you are able to secure the financing you need. And of course that's much more complex for multi-family properties.

My personal opinion is that it's better to start with single family homes. In fact, for most investors, I think it's best to stick fully with single-family properties.

I have some compelling reasons for why I only invest in single-family properties. I'll list them here, in no particular order.

To start with, it's much easier to finance single-family homes. The down payments are small enough that people with regular jobs can save up for them.

Plus, the underwriting process for single family financing is standard and straight forward. And we can get 30-year fixed-rate loans for every property in our portfolio. That's incredible.

The negotiation process is also very simple when we're talking about single-family homes. The price is largely based on comparable sales in the area, as well. That's not the case with multifamily properties. They are priced based on their financial performance—which means investors need to do a lot more due diligence up front. Then they'll likely need to negotiate with a skilled business person on the price.

And there's also the tenant to consider.

Simply put, people take more pride in their homes than their apartments in most places. Think about it this way…

Apartments tend to be just a place to crash that is close to all the action in the city. This attracts tenants who tend to be more transient. They often breeze in for twelve months and then move on.

As such, we will have far more tenant turnover with multifamily properties. And turnover is costly.

The rent stops coming in until we can get a new tenant into the unit. Before we can do that, we have to clean it and make a host of minor repairs that inevitably come from normal wear and tear. There's no way around that.

Meanwhile, I think renters are more likely to feel a connection to single-family homes. They are more likely to see them as a comfortable place of refuge. I think that's especially true now that such a large percentage of the population works remotely.

And my experience is that most single-family tenants will stay for at least two years. Some for much longer. This is what we want.

If our tenants renew with us year after year, then we don't have to turn over the property. That means we don't have to worry about cleaning or any of the minor repairs that accrue from normal wear and tear.

Meanwhile, the rent checks continue to roll in month after month. It's a much more relaxed experience for all parties involved.

Finally, a lot more can go wrong with multifamily units. That's true in terms of repairs—there's a lot more roof and a lot more appliances that owners are responsible for.

It's also true in terms of conflict and bad behavior.

There are a lot of headaches that can come from many different people living in the same housing units. And headaches are almost always bad for business.

At the end of the day it all comes down to what you want. What's your goal?

I set out to build a portfolio that produces $10,000 a month in passive income for me. That was my goal. And guess what?

It's fairly easy to get to that level with single family properties. And it doesn't take that long if we're committed to it. Plus, we can work up to $10,000 a month with very few headaches.

As I write, I think having $10,000 a month in passive income would equate to financial freedom for most people. Their rental income could cover their living expenses completely, so they wouldn't need a job anymore.

And here's the thing—I think most people can get to that point within six to twelve years. Just by building a portfolio of single-family rental properties.

Plus, there's nothing that says we have to stop growing our portfolio once we get to $10,000 a month. We can scale our business as much and as fast as we want to.

So, single family homes can get me where I want to go. And they can do so while keeping my life simple and headache-free. What more could I ask for?

That said, please keep in mind that single-family homes include duplexes, triplexes, and fourplexes. When it comes to financing and valuing real estate, those properties are treated the exact same. It's only when we get to five-unit properties that different "multi-family" rules apply.

At this point, we know how to analyze real estate investments. And we know how and why to establish specific investment criteria.

Equally critical—perhaps even more so—is your infrastructure. I would never buy a rental property in an area in which I did not have my core infrastructure in place.

I'm talking about professional infrastructure here…

Infrastructure

In every market in which we invest we need to have a team of trustworthy professionals. This includes a real estate agent, a property manager, a lender, and an insurance professional.

Our real estate agent is our "boots on the ground" in the market. At the base level, this is the person who can bring us deals that match our investment criteria. What's more, our real estate agent should have a thorough understanding of what's happening in the market—employment trends, new construction trends—those kinds of things.

Our property manager is the person or the company who will run our rental properties in that market for us. Once we buy a property, our property manager will take over. They will screen and place a tenant for us. This includes establishing the monthly rent, getting a signed lease agreement in place, and collecting the security deposit.

From there our property manager will collect the rent for us and deposit it into our bank account every single month. Talk about a service. Then our property manager will be our tenants' point of contact for everything. If something needs to be fixed in the house, the tenant will call our property manager.

For minor repairs, most property managers will handle it right away for us. This is spelled out in the property management agreement. As for larger repairs, our property manager will ask professionals to bid on the job. Then they will present us with the quotes. They won't move forward until we say so.

Most property managers can secure very competitive bids for any repair jobs we might have. That's because they have relationships with local contractors and tradesmen, and they send them repeat business over and over again. It's a virtuous circle of sorts.

Moving on to our lender, this is somebody licensed in the market we are targeting. This person can help us secure advantageous financing in a fast and efficient manner.

Often our real estate agent and property manager can provide us with lender referrals when we are just getting started. But most lenders are now licensed in many different states. So once we're comfortable with somebody, we may choose to finance our investments with them over and over again.

Finally, we need to have an insurance professional licensed in our target markets as well. This is a minor piece of the puzzle, but it becomes incredibly important to have a good agent if we ever need to file a claim.

These professionals make up our core infrastructure in every market where we invest. We build strong relationships with these people, and we rely on them to keep our investments performing well.

So, coming full circle here, the first step to finding potential real estate investments is to establish relationships with a real estate agent and/or a property manager in our target markets.

This begs the question—which markets should we target? And then how do we find a good real estate agent and property manager in those markets?

If we are investing in the same area in which we live, this is just a matter of going out and networking with local professionals. But I think it's far better to plug ourselves into existing real estate networks. After all, if investors have already built robust networks, why try to reinvent the wheel?

That's how I got started. I had a friend who had been investing in Dallas for ten years with great success. He introduced me to his agent and property manager, and they were more than happy to answer all my questions and concerns.

That gave me the confidence I needed to buy my first property in Dallas, and it worked out great. So I kept going.

However, there's a limit to this approach.

Real estate markets are not static. Just because we can buy properties in a particular market that are capable of producing great cash-on-cash returns one year doesn't mean we'll be able to do so the next. My experience in Dallas is a perfect example of this.

I started out with three new construction properties in Dallas. They each generated cash-on-cash returns well over 10 percent when I bought them. Then those returns moved substantially higher thanks to rent increases.

However, when I wanted to buy my fourth property, the numbers didn't work anymore. Housing prices in Dallas had skyrocketed… and rents hadn't caught up.

Not only could new construction properties not generate 10 percent returns, they could no longer generate a return at all. Cash flows had gone negative when I was looking for my fourth property.

This is why we need to have infrastructure in multiple real estate markets.

The easiest way to do that is to link up with companies who establish professional infrastructure across markets and then source properties for their clients.

There are a number of these companies out there, but I have only worked with one of them. And my experience has been fantastic. They focus on building long-term relationships with real estate investors. They offer free consulting calls. And they really do take the time to get to know each individual investor and their goals.

That enables the company to bring investors only properties that match their criteria perfectly. This includes providing investors with all the numbers needed to analyze the deal, as well as the pictures and neighborhood information needed to assess the property itself.

The benefit here is that we can suddenly consider properties in multiple markets at the same time. This allows us to constantly invest in those markets where the cash flow is best.

In other words, when the numbers in Dallas don't work anymore, we can jump to wherever the numbers work best. This opens us up to market arbitrage opportunities.

Market arbitrage occurs when real estate prices have boomed in one of our markets, but not another. When this happens, we can sell properties in the booming market to capture that price appreciation. Then we can use that money to buy multiple properties in the market where prices haven't risen so much.

This is a great way to scale our rental portfolio quickly.

And get this—there's a way to do this without paying capital gains taxes on the properties we sell. It's called a 1031 Exchange. It enables us to defer taxes on real estate indefinitely.

We'll talk about the 1031 Exchange and other advanced tax strategies in a later chapter. But before we get there, we have to talk about strategic financing.

Strategic Financing

Now that we have our criteria in place and we know how to source ideal real estate investments, we have to talk about strategic financing. I'll preface this by saying that I'm speaking from the American experience here. I don't have experience with financing in other countries.

I suspect that most Americans who are interested in real estate investments are familiar with conventional 30-year fixed-rate mortgages. These are typically the best financing options available to us as real-estate investors in the US.

For starters, the ability to lock in a rate for thirty years is absolutely incredible. This isn't even an option in most other countries.

By locking in a rate for thirty years we can put inflation to work for us instead of against us. To understand why, we have to understand the nature of inflation.

The term "inflation" is thrown around quite a bit today.

If you ask somebody what it means, they will probably tell you about rising prices. But if you ask them what causes inflation, can they give you a meaningful answer? In most cases, the answer is no.

As I mentioned earlier, I am sympathetic to the definition put forth by the Austrian School of Economics.[25] Inflation is the expansion of the money supply. It is the act of creating new money and injecting it into the economy.

If we speak from a dollar-centric point of view, inflation occurs when the Fed and the US Treasury pump new dollars into the system.

These dollars have to go somewhere. And wherever they go, we are likely to see rising prices follow. It's just supply-and-demand economics.

From this perspective, rising prices are the result of inflation. They are not inflation itself. What's really happening here is that the dollar is losing its purchasing power. This happens constantly.

[25] https://mises.org/library/defining-inflation

In fact, the US dollar has lost over 87 percent of its purchasing power since 1970. That's not my guess. That's based on the Fed's own data.[26]

This means that, generally speaking, thirteen cents in 1970 could buy what one dollar buys today. This is why nominal costs for nearly everything have gone up so much over time.

The financial media tries to mask this by comparing the dollar to other national currencies. If the dollar can suddenly buy more Euros or Yen, the media will go around talking about how strong the dollar is.

But that's only the case if you are in the market for Euros or Yen. It's a whole different story if you're looking for groceries or a new car.

What the media is really doing here is comparing how fast each currency is falling in relation to the other. They are basically timing the race to the bottom—which isn't helpful to any of us.

Here's the point…

As the dollar's purchasing power falls, the real value of all debt denominated in dollars also falls.

In other words, our debt burden shrinks over time. That's simply because we can pay the debt back with devalued dollars. Dollars that can buy less than they used to.

---

[26] https://fred.stlouisfed.org/series/CUUR0000SA0R#0

This is why locking in fixed mortgage payments on rental real estate is so powerful.

When we take out a 30-year fixed mortgage, the principal and interest payment never changes. What starts out as a reasonable monthly payment gets progressively easier to pay over time.

That said, did you know there is a limit to how many conventional loans any individual can take on?

As I write that limit is ten. We can only have ten conventional mortgages outstanding at any given time.

That's due to regulations around Fannie Mae and Freddie Mac. These are both government-sponsored entities.

And this brings us to the strategy piece—we should be very intentional with how we use our ten conventional mortgage slots.

For starters, if we are investing with a business partner, every mortgage we qualify for together will take up one slot for each of us. Thus, it's ideal to qualify for each mortgage independently, even if we are going in with a partner.

Let's look at it this way…

If my brother and I team up to build a rental portfolio together and we use both of our income and assets to qualify for each property, we can only obtain conventional loans for our first 10 properties.

However, if we are strategic about qualifying for each mortgage individually then we can secure conventional mortgages for our first 20 properties, even though we each have 50 percent ownership in all twenty of the properties.

That's because we can take on ten conventional mortgages each—so long as we can qualify for them individually. This may sound counter-intuitive at first, but the mortgage really has nothing to do with the property's ownership.

The mortgage company is going to record the property's deed in the name of the person who took out the conventional mortgage. That's going to happen at closing.

But guess what? We can always record a new deed later to change the property's legal ownership to whoever we want. I transferred the ownership of all my properties into my LLC's name several months after closing.

The point is, the mortgage doesn't have anything to do with the property's ownership.

So if we're investing with a partner, qualifying for each conventional mortgage independently is ideal. We don't have to each be on the loan.

But what if we're going it alone? In that case, it's probably best to save our ten conventional slots for larger properties.

Let's go back to our Birmingham-versus-Oklahoma City example from earlier to illustrate this:

Remember, the Birmingham property was priced at just $128,000. But the Oklahoma City property cost $325,000.

If we are building a portfolio of diverse properties like this, it makes sense to go with conventional financing for the larger properties while working with a lender who specializes in asset-based loans for the smaller units.

That's because asset-based lenders typically cannot offer interest rates that are as low as conventional mortgages. They are beholden to their investors who are going to buy the mortgages from them. So the investors can dictate what rates they are comfortable with.

As a result, rental properties financed with asset-based loans will likely produce less cash flow each month. That's why I prefer to save my conventional slots for larger properties.

That said, there are asset-based lenders out there who can do 30-year fixed-rate mortgages. The rate may be a little higher, but whenever possible I always want to fix my rate for 30 years.

Plus, asset-based loans aren't subjected to the same underwriting guidelines as conventional loans. That makes the qualifying process much easier.

So what are asset-based loans?

Simply put, they are loans where the lender underwrites the property itself, rather than us as borrowers.

The lenders look at market rents and they determine whether the property can produce enough income to cover all expenses with a reasonable cushion left over. If that's the case, the property can qualify for the loan.

Asset-based lenders still run our credit report and verify that we have the down payment funds we need to close on the property, but that's about it. They don't require us to submit tax returns, pay stubs, and all the other documents that conventional lenders require.

So these are a fantastic option for us as investors, especially if we're self-employed. Conventional lenders have a harder time with self-employed folks.

Still, as investors we would be better served going through the tougher underwriting process in exchange for cheaper money and higher returns. So let's talk more about how to maximize our conventional loan slots.

A minute ago, I used the example of partnering with my brother to get 20 conventional loans between us. What happens when we hit the limit?

Well, what if we bring our spouses into the game? If we can structure their finances so that they can each qualify individually, there's another twenty slots. That would allow us to finance our first forty properties with conventional loans.

And here's the thing – our spouses don't have to be involved in the real estate business at all for this to work. We just need them to qualify for the loan. That's it.

So let's talk briefly about what it takes to qualify for conventional mortgages…

First off, all lenders require a down payment of at least 20 percent for rental properties. And generally the underwriters want to see that our down payment funds have been sitting in a bank account or an investment account for at least two months.

In addition, all lenders will want to see that we have reserves above and beyond what's needed for the down payment and closing costs. Keeping at least six months' worth of reserves is always a good idea.

As for our credit score, borrowers with a score above 740 will typically get the best terms. And most lenders are willing to work with borrowers who have a score above 620, though the rate offered won't be as good.

Finally, the underwriters usually require borrowers to have a debt-to-income ratio below 36 percent. Some lenders will go up to 45 percent, though.

The debt to income ratio—often called DTI—refers to the total amount of our monthly debt payments divided by our gross monthly income. There are plenty of debt-to-income calculators floating around online to see where we stand.

Keep in mind though, rental properties are treated differently in the DTI calculation. If a property produces positive cash flow, that cash flow is attributed as income to the borrower. If a property breaks even, both the debt and income associated with it are ignored. And if a property loses money each month, that negative cash flow factors into the borrower's debt service calculation.

To summarize, to qualify for a conventional mortgage we need to have sufficient funds to cover the down payment and maintain a reasonable reserve. We also need to have an acceptable credit score. And we need a DTI that meets the lender's criteria.

Of course, we will be required to provide all kinds of documentation to prove our creditworthiness. Pay stubs... bank statements... investment statements... mortgage statements... lease agreements... tax returns... insurance statements... we have to fork all of it over. It's somewhat of a tedious process that could take about a month to complete. But it will become much easier once we have established a relationship with lenders in our market.

The key thing to understand with this is that every lender is beholden to Fannie Mae and Freddie Mac underwriting guidelines if they want to sell the mortgage to an investor. And this is something nearly every lender wants to do.

So please don't get frustrated with your loan processor as you go through underwriting. They are just checking all the boxes they need to check. And I promise they don't like coming back to us with more questions any more than we like answering them. Let's be sure to treat them well.

All right, now we've got strategic financing down. Let's move on and talk about business structure and management.

Key Points

- Having pre-defined investment criteria is the difference between experts and amateur investors
- Investment criteria takes all the guesswork out of analysis

- For rental real estate, our investment criteria should include:
    - The types of properties we want to buy
    - Our minimum acceptable cash-on-cash return
    - Our desired allocation to newer versus older properties
    - The markets in which we would like to invest
- Single-family homes are easier to analyze and finance than multi-family properties
- We have less tenant turnover with single family homes compared to multi-family
- Single-family properties can get us to $10,000 a month in extra income
- We should only buy properties in markets where we have infrastructure in place
- Our infrastructure includes: real estate agents, property managers, lenders, and insurance professionals
- The best way to invest in real estate is through existing networks that already have infrastructure in place
- Fixed 30-year mortgages put inflation to work for us
- That's important because the US dollar has lost over 87 percent of its purchasing power since 1970
- As the dollar's purchasing power falls, the real value of debt denominated in dollars also falls
- That means our mortgage payments get easier to pay over time
- The limit to how many conventional mortgages an individual can take out is currently ten
- We need to be intentional with how we use our ten conventional mortgages
- The alternative to conventional financing is what's called asset-based financing
- Conventional financing typically offers a better rate than asset-based financing

CHAPTER ELEVEN

BUSINESS STRUCTURE AND MANAGEMENT

At this point we know how to build our infrastructure, determine our investment criteria, analyze properties, and then finance them correctly. Now we have to talk about how to structure our business and manage our operations.

Let's start with this: every rental property we own should be run through an LLC. That may sound overwhelming at first, but it's not nearly as complicated as it first seems.

For those who may not be familiar with them, LLCs are limited liability companies. These are pass-through business entities that, if used properly, can reduce an individual's tax burden and provide asset protection in the event of a lawsuit.

We'll talk about using LLCs to manage our finances and reduce our taxes in this chapter and the next. Then we will talk about using LLCs to protect our assets in chapter thirteen. That's a completely separate discussion with different action steps.

For tax purposes, the LLC's net income or loss flows through to the individuals who own the entity.

For example, if an LLC made $10,000 in a given year, that $10,000 would be taxed as income for the individuals who own the LLC. And the reverse is true also. If an LLC loses $10,000 in a given year, that loss would flow through to the LLC owners' personal tax returns.

Now, there are specific rules regarding how pass-through losses are treated. We'll talk about taxes more in the next chapter. For now, let's stick with the fundamentals of LLCs.

LLCs are incredibly flexible. If we are investing with a business partner, we can structure the LLC to be treated as a partnership. Then we can designate how much of the company each partner owns.

I have partnered with my brother on a number of real estate deals. We always go in 50–50. That means we both put up 50 percent of the down payment and we agree to split income and expenses right down the middle. As such, we set ourselves as 50 percent owners of the LLC.

But we could just as easily decide to go 60–40 percent… or 75–25 percent… or 96–4 percent… whatever makes sense for our circumstances. There are no limits here.

This dynamic is just the same regardless of how many partners there are in the LLC.

For example, we could have three partners with an ownership structure of, say, 40 percent for the first, 40 percent for the second, and 20 percent for the third. There are no limits or restrictions regarding the number of members or their ownership level when it comes to LLCs.

But what if we are investing without a partner?

In that case, we can structure our LLC to be taxed as an S-Corporation. This simply requires filing form 2553 with the Internal Revenue Service (IRS). We would do that after establishing our LLC and obtaining its Tax ID number.

Before we get to the how-to specifics, the beautiful thing here is that running our rental properties through LLCs puts the tax code on our side.

That's because LLCs are taxed on their net income, not their gross income. That means we can deduct all our business expenses throughout the year and only pay taxes on whatever's leftover.

This opens the door to a wealth of tax planning opportunities that a good CPA can help us capitalize on. And if we implement the tax strategies we will discuss in the next chapter, we shouldn't have to pay any taxes on our rental income. Real estate is an incredibly tax-advantaged asset.

To illustrate, let's compare this to W2 employees.

Employees are taxed on their gross income. And those taxes come right out of their paycheck before they ever see the money. As a result, employees are forced to pay taxes first, then they can use whatever money is leftover as they see fit.

With LLCs it's the exact opposite. LLCs get to use the money first, then they pay taxes on whatever is left over.

All right, let's dig into the specifics a little bit more.

First, I'm going to describe the traditional approach to structuring real estate investments with LLCs. I want you to understand this first… then we'll talk about a better approach.

The traditional approach is to set up at least one LLC in every state in which we buy real estate. For tax purposes we can run as many rental properties through the same LLC as we like. However, if we are sued because of something that happens at one of our properties, the plaintiff could go after assets associated with every property under the same LLC.

For this reason it's best not to have too much value operating under the same entity. In states that allow Series LLCs, this is easy to address. We'll talk about this more in a few minutes.

The process of setting up an LLC is simple. We can do it right from the state's Secretary of State website. Best of all, there's no approval process. We just provide the information requested and then we receive a Certificate of Approval from the Secretary of State.

Once registered with the state, we would then apply for an Employer Identification Number (EIN) from the IRS. Again this is a simple process we can do right online.

That said, those who don't want to deal with setting up their LLCs manually can always hire an entity specialist to do it all for them.

Legal Zoom is the most common company providing this service. I also have an LLC specialist that provides the same services Legal Zoom offers, and more.

Once we have our LLC established, we can take the Certificate of Formation documents and our EIN documents down to the bank to open up a bank account for the LLC. This is critical—make sure the rent always goes to the LLC's bank account. We should not deposit rent into our personal accounts.

I also highly recommend opening up a new credit card for each LLC. This makes managing the business easy. Personally, I put all business expenses on the LLC's credit card. Then I pay it down when the rent comes in each month.

Unlike personal credit cards, I'm not overly worried about paying my business cards to zero every month. That's because the finance charges associated with credit card balances are tax deductible when run through an LLC.

So I don't mind paying a little bit in interest every month—especially when I'm just getting a new LLC off the ground. I would much rather make sure that I have a strong cash reserve on hand at all times in case an unexpected repair comes up.

Next we need to talk about bookkeeping. Bookkeeping is the process of documenting every single transaction that occurs within the business.

We can hire a professional bookkeeper to do this for us. Or we can do it ourselves using accounting software like QuickBooks or even spreadsheet software like Excel.

I asked my CPA if he had a preference between QuickBooks and Excel. He told me he is just happy when his clients actually keep up with their books. It didn't matter to him what format the bookkeeping was in.

So I do all my bookkeeping in Excel. I've got a simple system that's intuitive to me. Here's what it looks like:

XYZ LLC					
Date					
			PropertyA 2/01	PropertyB 2/01	Property C 2/01
BB&T Checking:	$3,195.67		$181,041.47	$194,826.68	$211,810.71
Series One Checking	$9,470.12				
Series Two Checking	$10,205.91				
Series Three Checking	$100.00				
Cumulative Balance:	**$22,971.70**				
Credit Card:	$2,420.99	*$17,579.01*			
Monthly Rent	$7,823.00		Revenue:	$97,597.87	
Mortgage	$4,856.20		Expenses:	$66,258.67	
Management Fee	$625.84		Net Income:	$31,339.20	
Cash Flow	**$2,340.96**				
Mortgage Interest	$23,784.97				
Taxes & Insurance	$21,516.49				
Utilities	$1,990.11				
Maintenance	$993.64				
Professional Services	$15,146.92				
Meals	$1,288.52				
Travel	$1,298.66				
Education	$0.00				
Finance Charges	$231.41				
Postage	$7.95				
Closing Costs					
Total	**$66,258.67**				

Here we can see the main tab in my spreadsheet. I call it "Financials." It gives me a snapshot of where each company is at any given time. Let's walk through this section-by-section real quick.

In the upper left hand corner I list my checking account and my credit card balances. This is a Series LLC with a separate bank account set up for each independent Series—we'll talk more about that in a few minutes.

What I want to share with you first is my personal reserve strategy for this particular LLC.

Each of the checking account balances you see here built up over time exclusively from rental cash flow. I deposited $100 of my personal money into each account to start it up… and that's it. I never put in any additional money from a personal account.

To me, that's what makes rental real estate so much fun. I started with $100 in each account and that grew into nearly $23,000—just from rent checks coming in each month. My goal in this particular market is to build a cash reserve of $10,000 in each of these accounts.

These were new construction properties when I bought them, so I'm very confident that $10,000 per account will be plenty to cover any repairs that pop up for the next five to ten years.

I may adjust my reserve requirements upward as these properties age, but for now I distribute out any funds above $10,000 to my personal account. And I use these funds to help me with down payments on new properties. I'll show you a distribution example in just a minute.

But first—to the right of my bank account balances I list my mortgage balances and when the next payments are due. In this case, I have three properties—dubbed Property A, Property B, and Property C. And my next payment for each is due February 1.

Then look at the next grouping of figures just below. I list my cumulative monthly rent, mortgage payments, and property management fees. This shows me that my monthly cash flow for these three properties is $2,341 a month.

To the right of those numbers I am tracking my annual revenue and expenses. As we can see, this snapshot shows that on this particular date, my revenue for the year was $97,598 and my expenses were just over $66,259. That gave me a net income of $31,339.

At the bottom of the spreadsheet I'm tracking a breakdown of each expense category. These include mortgage interest, taxes and insurance, utilities, maintenance, professional services, meals, travel, education, finance charges, postage, and closing costs. This allows me to see in real-time exactly where my expenses are going.

Before we go any further, I need to point something out. Do you see that net income number of $31,339? That's not what will flow through to me personally as taxable income.

Instead, I will show a loss for tax purposes because I will take accelerated depreciation on my newest property. I haven't finalized this with my CPA as I write this, but I should be able to write off over $40,000 in depreciation in this particular year. That will effectively convert my $31,339 in income into roughly a $9,000 loss for tax purposes.

Think about that. I made over $31,000… that's money which flowed into my bank accounts. Yet I can legally report a loss on my tax return. That means I will owe no taxes on my rental income.

That's how powerful the tax benefits of real estate are. We'll talk about that in much more detail in the next chapter. But before we get there, let's look at one of my monthly bookkeeping tabs.

Expenses								
Account	***Amount***							
Mortgage Interest	$2,070.97							
Taxes & Insurance	$1,898.63							
Utilities								
Maintenance								
Professional Svcs	$936.48							
Meals	$320.06							
Travel	$1,222.96							
Education								
Finance Charges	$15.94							
Postage								
Total								
Transactions			**Series One**			**Series Two**		
Management Fee	$200.00	12/31/21	Management Fee	$208.48	12/31/21	Management Fee	$228.00	12/31/21
Mtg Interest	$618.80	12/10/21	Mtg Interest	$679.92	12/10/21	Mtg Interest	$772.25	12/10/21
Mtg Taxes & Ins	$587.53	12/10/21	Mtg Taxes & Ins	$646.79	12/10/21	Mtg Taxes & Ins	$664.31	12/10/21
Hyatt Place Roanoke	$115.57	5-Dec	Bookkeeping	$100.00	12/13/21	Bookkeeping	$100.00	12/17/21
Nobies	$320.06	6-Dec						
JW Mariott	$285.39	7-Dec						
Roanoke Regional Air	$27.00	12/7/21						
Rocket Limo	$795.00	12/7/21						
Finance Charge	$15.94	12/16/21				**Distribution to Mike	$2,500.00	9-Dec
Bookkeeping	$100.00	12/17/21				**Distribution to Joe	$2,500.00	9-Dec
Income			**Series One**			**Series Two**		
Account	***Amount***		***Account***	***Amount***		***Account***	***Amount***	
Rent - 256 Painted Trl	$2,500.00		Rent - 289 Cisco	$2,606.00		Rent - 264 Painted Trl	$2,850.00	
Total	**$7,956.00**							

Financials | December | November | October | September | August | July | June | May | April | March | February | January | +

Here you can see the same expense categories that we're tracking on the main spreadsheet. In fact, that main spreadsheet is pulling the numbers from these monthly tabs to give me my running totals.

And at the bottom of this spreadsheet I list every single transaction the business made for the month. These are the transactions that feed into the main expense categories at the top of the tab.

For example, I pay property management fees and bookkeeping fees for each property every month. Those feed into the Professional Services expense category. I also did some travel for the business this particular month—those expenses feed into my travel and meals expense categories.

Look underneath the Series Two transactions. There you can see two distributions—one to my brother Mike and one to me.

Mike and I are each 50 percent owners of Series Two. And since the checking account had grown to $15,000, we decided to distribute $5,000 out to ourselves personally. We used those funds as earnest money to get a new property out in Kansas City under contract.

Please note that distributions like this are not a business expense. That's because the net income of the business flows through to us individually at the end of the year anyway. So distributing money to the LLC's owners does not impact the LLC's net income.

The key takeaway here is that bookkeeping is simple. It can even be fun.

The main thing is to stay on top of your books at least once a month. Personally, I spend ten or twenty minutes updating my bookkeeping spreadsheet every Friday.

If we stay on top of our books like this, we will always be in control of our LLC's finances. And this enables us to do advanced tax planning with a CPA at various points through the year. That ensures we are running our real estate investments in a way that's as tax efficient as possible.

We will make a template of our bookkeeping spreadsheet available to everyone who reads this book. Please see the 'Key Points' section at the end of this chapter to find out how to access it.

That said, we have to talk about Series LLCs now. Remember when I said that you needed to have an LLC set up in each state you invest in?

Well, there is a way around that. If we establish a Series LLC in one of those states where they are treated well, we can use that Series LLC to acquire property in other states.

A Series LLC is basically an umbrella LLC. There's a "parent" company that's over top of each independent series within the Series LLC. I'll explain with a real world example…

I have two Series LLCs. One in Alabama. And one in Texas.

The Texas LLC holds the rental properties that my brother and I partner on. We started it with three rental properties in Dallas, and we set up a separate series for each. They are creatively named Series One, Series Two, and Series Three.

These independent series (Series One/Series Two/Series Three) are treated like their own LLC for tax and asset protection purposes. However, their financials flow into the parent LLC's tax return. That way we only have to file a single tax return each year.

So we started the Series LLC in Texas with three properties in Dallas. When it came time for us to acquire our fourth property together, property values in Dallas had gone up so much that the numbers no longer worked for rental properties in the area. That's because home prices appreciated far faster than rents. So we couldn't buy a new property with cash flow that fit our criteria.

However, we did find a new construction property in Kansas City, MO that matched our criteria.

Originally we thought we would need to set up a new LLC in Missouri for that property. But we talked with both our CPA and our asset protection attorney, and they both agreed that we could set up Series Four within our Texas Series LLC and then register Series Four as a foreign entity with the Missouri Secretary of State.

Registering a foreign entity works a lot like setting up a new LLC. It's easy to do.

The benefit here is that we don't have to create a new LLC for properties in a new state. We just create a new series and register it as a foreign entity in the property's state.

That means we don't need to appoint another registered agent for the new property. And we won't have to file yet another tax return each year. Instead, all we need to do is set up a new bank account in the name of Series Four. I see this as a neat little hack. I've done the same thing with my Series LLC in Alabama also.

There is one nuance to this, however.

Each state has different fees for registering a foreign entity. So it's a good idea to check into that first to determine if it makes sense to go this route.

And as always, please discuss this idea with your own team of professionals just to make sure that it will work for your situation. To the best of my knowledge this will work for pretty much anyone. But I'm not a CPA or attorney—so all I can give is generalized information.

Key Points

- Every rental property should be run through an LLC
- LLCs are pass-through entities that can reduce our tax burden and provide asset protection
- An LLCs net income or loss flows through to the owners' tax return(s)
- LLCs are incredibly flexible with regards to ownership structure
- LLCs can be taxed as a partnership or as an S-Corporation
- We should set up a bank account and a credit card for our LLCs
- Rent should always go to the LLC's bank account—not our personal account
- We should be diligent with bookkeeping for our LLCs

- We should also have a strategy for building cash reserves within each LLC
- We can use depreciation to offset any net income generated from rents received
- Series LLCs make it easy to manage multiple rental properties across different states

Action to take: We are making our bookkeeping template available to everyone who reads this book. If you would like to grab your copy, you can find it right here: https://beyondthenestegg.com/extras/

CHAPTER TWELVE

SHATTER THE GLASS CEILING

We have to start this chapter by acknowledging something that often goes unsaid…

In every developed industrial country there is a glass ceiling of sorts hanging over top of the middle class. This is certainly true in the US. Here's what I mean...

When we add up all of the taxes across all levels of government, the average middle class person pays at least half of their income out in taxes each year.

It starts with the taxes that are typically withheld from our paychecks every two weeks. The Federal Income Tax… State Income Tax… Social Security Tax… the Medicare Tax—these taxes are each taken right out of our paycheck before we ever see the money.

Then we have to pay sales taxes on every good or service we purchase. And we pay excise taxes on things like gasoline and alcoholic beverages. We also have to pay property taxes on any real estate we own. Then we pay taxes and registration fees on our vehicles.

These are taxes that virtually all middle class people pay—year in, year out.

Then if we happen to make any money on our investments, we're required to pay the capital gains tax on our earnings. Unless we defer those gains through a qualified retirement account. If that's the case, we'll be on the hook for normal income taxes on our money down the road.

If we were to add up the dollar amount of all these taxes each year, I bet it would equate to roughly half of our income. Which begs the question—how does one get ahead this way?

That's the glass ceiling. Those who simply work a W2 job and save their money in retirement plans are pitting themselves against the tax code every step of the way.

In this chapter, we're going to talk about how to shatter the glass ceiling. One of the best ways to do this is to leverage the advanced tax benefits that come with rental real estate. This is where the asset class truly shines.

I mentioned briefly in the last chapter that one of my LLCs generated over $31,000 in net income for me in a particular year. However, I used the tax code to write off over $40,000 in accelerated depreciation. That converted my $31,000 gain into a $9,000 loss for tax purposes.

I can't overstate how powerful this is. My real estate investments made a nice chunk of money—money that flowed directly into my bank accounts. But I was taxed as though my investments lost money. That's the name of the game. That's how we break through the glass ceiling.

Now, I want to stop right here and address a common reaction to this. I know some people will read this and think—*that's not fair*! *Shouldn't everybody have to pay the same taxes on their income*?

Here's the thing—anybody who pays taxes in the United States can do exactly what I did and get the exact same tax treatment. I simply used the tax code as it is written. Anybody else can do the same.

You see, the tax code is 100 percent fair.

If you follow the rules, you get the designated result no matter who you are. No matter what your net worth is. No matter what your political beliefs are. It doesn't matter. The code is the same for everybody.

Sure, there are plenty of things about the tax code that I would rather be different. W2 wage earners absolutely get the short-end of the stick. And that's most people. This is a big reason why so many people are stuck in the rat race.

Unfortunately, there's nothing we can do about that. We can't change the tax code.

All we can do is operate according to the rules as they exist. And as it turns out, the rules are designed to incentivize certain activities. That's why real estate is favored.

As we know, real estate is a major economic driver in the United States. A lot of people derive their income from real estate. Real estate agents, mortgage brokers, title companies, insurance companies, appraisers—they all get paid every time somebody buys a house.

What's more, small investors like me make far better landlords than the government and the massive multinational corporations. That's because we treat our tenants exceptionally well. We ensure that our properties are in good shape. And we respond quickly any time there is a problem.

For many of us, we do this because we genuinely care about our fellow humans. We treat them the way we like to be treated ourselves.

And even for those small investors who maybe aren't as benevolent—well, they still can't afford to not treat their tenants well. Happy tenants provide stable cash flow. Angry tenants provide headaches and losses.

This is why the US tax code encourages people to invest in real estate. As real estate investors, we are providing a valuable service to the marketplace. And we're taking on all the risk. If something goes wrong with our properties, it's on us to fix it.

Now let's talk about some advanced tax planning. We'll start with real estate's big tax advantage—depreciation.

Depreciation is simply an accounting method that allocates the cost of a physical asset over its useful life expectancy. The IRS says that single family homes have a useful life of 27.5 years. Thus, real estate investors can depreciate 3.636 percent of the property's value every single year.

In other words, depreciation allows investors to expense a small percentage of future repairs every single year… even though they haven't occurred yet. In this way, depreciation is really just a phantom loss. It's a loss on paper for tax purposes.

For example, if we own a property worth $100,000, we can write off $3,636 in depreciation every year. This reduces our taxable income, even though we never incurred a real expense.

Not too shabby, right? Well, let's kick it into hyper-drive.

What I just described is called straight-line depreciation. It's what happens by default. Your CPA or tax professional will assume straight-line depreciation for your properties unless you take accelerated depreciation.

As the name implies, accelerated depreciation allows you to write off a larger percentage of your asset faster. Here's how it works...

When it comes to real estate, the tax code acknowledges that certain parts of the home wear out faster than others. If we do a detailed analysis and document the specific value of each part of the home—how much are the windows worth... the flooring... plumbing... HVAC... appliances... and so forth—if we break out the value of each specific item, the tax code says we can write off a percentage of certain items much faster than the standard 27.5 years.

Here's the best part—we don't need to do this analysis ourselves. We can hire a professional to do a cost segregation report to accomplish this for us. And for normal single family homes, the cost segregation report can be done online. Nobody needs to physically visit the property.

I use a company called KBKG to do my cost segregation studies. They charge $300 per study, and all they need is for me to fill out specific details on the property. I get most of these details right from the appraisal.

At tax time, I simply forward the cost segregation report to my CPA and he works out the rest. It's far more simple than it sounds.

By the way, I'll provide you with a link to KBKG's cost segregation services in the Key Points section below.

Think about it this way… a $300 report allowed me to write off $40,000 for tax purposes in the example I used above. That sounds too good to be true, right?

Well, there is a nuance here. Unless we qualify as a Real Estate Professional, we can only use this accelerated depreciation to offset our yearly income for the given property.

In other words, the accelerated depreciation takes our net income for that property down to zero and no farther. Whatever depreciation was not used is recorded as a "carry-over loss." And carry-over losses can only be used to offset future passive income.

That in itself is an amazing benefit. It means we will likely not pay any taxes on our rental properties for many years... if ever. However, it can get even better.

If we can qualify as a Real Estate Professional, we can use our accelerated depreciation to reduce all taxable income, regardless of where it comes from. In other words, we could use it to offset all other income sources, including W2 income or revenue from other businesses.

Here's why that's important…

If we are consistently buying properties every year, it's likely that we will accumulate $20,000 or more in carry-over losses for each property. If we are a real estate professional, these losses will flow through and reduce our taxable income by the same amount—not just our income from the properties.

The end result is a much bigger tax refund each year. If we are wise, we will use those big tax refunds to buy even more real estate, thus creating a cycle that fuels itself.

So how do we qualify as a Real Estate Professional?

This is an IRS designation. It has nothing to do with being a licensed real estate agent or broker.

Instead, the IRS says that a Real Estate Professional is someone who spends at least 750 hours working on their real estate business every year *AND* they do not spend more time doing any other income-producing activity. In other words, real estate has to be their primary business.

So to qualify as a Real Estate Professional, we must log 750 hours of work on real estate in the given year. And we must show that we didn't spend more time on another job or business.

That's it. We just need to document our real estate hours in a spreadsheet or a notebook. There's no official qualification process. Of course, if we were ever audited then the first thing the IRS would want to do is go through our real estate log. As such, it's important to be diligent and honest with regards to our hours.

One tip that my CPA gave me for this is to document everything by hand in a notebook every week. That way it's obvious that we keep a running log of our hours while we are on the go. If we're in an audit, we don't want the IRS wondering if we simply created a new spreadsheet and stayed up half the night making up our numbers.

Speaking of hours, if we do the math, 750 hours a year is only 14 hours a week. That's not daunting. But it's also a high enough bar to where we do have to do some real work in order to qualify.

So what kind of activities can we use to build hours to qualify as a Real Estate Professional?

We can spend time each week doing our own bookkeeping, researching listings, and talking to real estate agents and property managers. Time can also be spent going out and viewing properties. It doesn't matter if we never buy any of these properties… just educating ourselves on the local market is something a real estate professional would do.

These are simple things that anyone can start doing right away, but it will be hard to get 750 hours a year if they're the *only* things that are done.

The easiest way to get the rest of the hours we need is to manage a property or two ourselves in our local area. This could be a long-term rental if we invest locally. It could also be a short-term rental—an AirBNB or VRBO—if we do not buy long-term rentals locally.

What if neither of those options are feasible in our area? In that case, it's time to get creative.

One idea is to buy a small house or building and lease it to a small business for office space. This could be our own small business or somebody's else's. Then we could be the property manager for that space. We could clean it weekly and handle all routine upkeep, just as we would with a short-term rental.

As you can see, there's certainly work involved if we want to qualify as a Real Estate Professional. But if we stay on top of it, fourteen hours a week isn't too hard to handle.

And that brings us to a neat little hack…

I'm sure many people reading this book are W2 employees. They are reading this and thinking—*well, I've got a full-time job. That rules me out.*

And they would be correct. If you work a full-time job, you won't be able to qualify as a Real Estate Professional. But guess what?

If you are married, only one spouse has to qualify as a Real Estate Professional for both spouses to get the tax benefits.

So even if you work full time and make all the investments, if your spouse can get 750 hours and not spend more time on another business, he or she can get you to the promised land. Then you can use accelerated depreciation to offset your W2 income.

And that scenario is especially powerful, because your employer will withhold far more money on each paycheck then you will end up owing in taxes. As a result, you will get some monster refunds come tax time.

This is the holy grail for any households who generate active income—either from a salaried job or for a non-real estate business. If we have active income, we can use our real estate investments to reduce our tax burden in a major way. That's how we shatter the glass ceiling.

Here's the key—we need to work very closely with a skilled CPA if we want to use the Real Estate Professional designation. Our CPA can advise us on the best practices we need to follow. And they can probably give us some tips for things we can do to get the hours we need as well.

Please don't try to implement these advanced tax strategies alone. Work with a professional who understands the ins and outs of the tax code as it pertains to real estate.

And for those who are in a situation where qualifying as a Real Estate Professional just isn't feasible—no worries. You can still use your depreciation to eliminate the taxes that you would otherwise owe on your rental income.

For many of us the goal is to build a rental portfolio that's big enough to replace our active income. Once we're there, qualifying as a real estate professional will be much easier.

The bottom line is that real estate is an incredibly tax-advantaged asset. It's a legitimate tax shelter here in the US. And that's baked right into the US tax code. There's no need to stretch the law or chase exotic schemes. We can simply utilize depreciation and deductions in strategic ways to reduce our taxes significantly.

And remember, anybody can do this. All we are talking about here is following the tax code as it's written.

Okay, let's move on to our lesson on asset protection.

Key Points

- In every developed country there is a glass ceiling over the middle class
- When we add up all the levels of taxes, the average person pays at least half their income out in taxes each year
- Advanced tax strategies can shatter the glass ceiling
- Anybody can leverage the tax code—it's not reserved for insiders
- The US tax code encourages people to invest in real estate
- Real estate's big tax advantage is depreciation
- There are ways to accelerate depreciation to enhance our tax benefits
- By default we can only use depreciation to offset income tied to the same property
- If we qualify as a Real Estate Professional per IRS guidelines, we can unlock this depreciation to offset other forms of income
- To qualify as a Real Estate Professional, we must spend at least 750 hours working on our real estate business and we cannot spend more time on any other income-producing activity
- With these incredible tax advantages, there's absolutely no reason to stretch the law or chase exotic tax schemes… we can simply follow the tax code as it's written

Action to take: You can learn more about KBKG's cost segregation services at the following link: https://beyondthenestegg.com/extras/

CHAPTER THIRTEEN

BULLETPROOF ASSET PROTECTION

"An investment in knowledge pays the best interest." -Benjamin Franklin

This quote speaks to why we need to be diligent with our asset-protection practices.

When we talk about asset protection, we're talking about strategies to protect our assets from lawsuits. Obviously, the rate of return our assets provide for us will not matter if someone is able to take our assets away from us.

And make no mistake about it—there are people out there who are more than happy to do so. The seeds of envy have been sown throughout the western world. That's why it's critical that we take steps to protect what we've worked so hard to build.

When we talk about lawsuits, we're talking about frivolous suits here.

If we maintain our properties and treat our tenants right, then our chances of being sued are small. But it should be noted that you never know when somebody is going to fall down on the sidewalk in front of your property and see it as a ticket to come after you and your assets.

As such, when we talk about asset protection, understand it has nothing to do with operations, taxes, or finances. Asset protection is strictly about ensuring that somebody can't sue us and take our money and our assets away for no reason.

In fact, the asset-protection strategies we discuss here will make it much more difficult for someone to sue us in the first place. That's because lawyers do their homework before accepting any case. When they do their homework on someone implementing these strategies, they know that their chances of getting much out of it will be small.

That said, I am not an attorney or a legal professional. Nothing in the lesson should be construed as personalized legal advice. Please consult a legal professional if you need any specific guidance.

Most of what we talk about in this lesson will concern LLCs, warranty deeds, and walling off our properties correctly. Before we get started, there are a few minor tips I would like to share with you first.

It starts with this—we shouldn't associate all of our accounts with our home address, personal cell phone number, and personal email address. Doing this makes us very transparent on the internet for those who know how to do a little sleuth work.

I know this sounds like a simple thing, but how many people tie all of their accounts to the same home address, the same phone number, and the same email address?

We tend to think that this is what we're supposed to do. But we shouldn't.

Instead, we should use different addresses and numbers for different accounts. This adds a little bit of resiliency to our digital footprint.

To do this, I use a service offered by Traveling Mailbox. This is a company that maintains physical mailing addresses in a number of states, and it will accept mail on our behalf at these addresses.

I have Traveling Mailbox addresses in a few different states. And I associate these addresses with various accounts. I rarely tie my physical address to any account.

When mail goes to one of those addresses, Traveling Mailbox simply uploads a picture of it to my online portal. Then I tell them what to do with it. I can ask them to open and scan the mail so that I can view images of it. Or I can ask them to forward my mail to another address, perhaps my physical address. Or I can ask them to shred and delete the mail without opening it.

It's a wonderful service, and it allows us to use several different physical addresses for different accounts.

As for alternative phone numbers, I use a smartphone app called MySudo. This app allows you to claim phone numbers with various area codes for yourself. Then, any calls or texts going to those numbers come right to your cell phone.

The beauty here is that the MySudo numbers are not registered to us personally. To my knowledge, there's no way for somebody to trace those numbers back to our device.

As for email addresses, I use ProtonMail to create different email addresses for different purposes. The great thing about doing this through ProtonMail is that I can manage all of my emails from the same account. And ProtonMail gives me the option to send encrypted emails very easily.

These are each relatively minor steps we can take, but they can do wonders for asset protection. That's because they make our digital footprint murky. Any lawyer doing sleuth work on us would have a hard time piecing the picture together. And that means they are far less likely to sue us in the first place.

The next piece of the asset protection puzzle is insurance.

As real estate investors, we should absolutely carry an umbrella insurance policy covering at least a few million dollars. These policies cover us personally, and they would kick in to cover any damages awarded in a lawsuit against us—up to our coverage limit, that is.

For example, if we are sued for $1 million and we lose the case, our umbrella insurance would pay out that $1 million to the plaintiff. Nothing comes out of our own pocket. These policies are cheap, and we can typically bundle them with our personal home and auto insurance to get a discount.

And keep in mind, these policies should grow as our assets grow. When we're just getting started, a $1 million umbrella policy is probably plenty. But as we build our assets, we should increase our insurance coverage.

That said, an umbrella policy does not cover our rental properties once we move them into an LLC. So let's talk about how to use LLCs correctly to maintain strong asset protection.

The number one rule when it comes to asset protection is to treat every property or groups of properties as their own independent business. We do this by having a separate LLC, bank account, and credit card for each property or groups of properties. Then we keep everything isolated and segregated.

Properties in different LLCs have nothing to do with one another. They certainly shouldn't be transferring money back and forth to each other. We should never commingle funds.

If we need to move money, then we can simply transfer the funds from one LLC's account to our personal bank account. We record that as a Distribution. From there we can transfer that money from our personal account to another LLC's account. We record this as a Contribution.

The key here is that the money going into the second LLC's account came from us personally. It did not come from the first LLC. Here's why that's important…

If we are sued because of something that happened at one property, we need to be able to demonstrate that all our other properties are independent of it. If we have money flying back and forth between accounts, that's a hard claim to make. But if each property is isolated in its own business dealings—

money never moves from one property to another directly—we should be safe.

So that begs the question—should we use a separate LLC and bank account for each and every property?

And the answer is... it depends. It can become tedious to manage a bunch of LLCs and bank accounts. Not to mention the fact that we have to file tax returns for each LLC.

So there may be cases where we group two or three properties together under one LLC to simplify it a little bit. The number to keep in mind here is our equity in each property. That's what's at risk. If we have two or three newer properties that we only have a small amount of equity in, those are probably fine to group together.

However, if we group properties within the same LLC, we should be careful not to keep too much cash in that LLC's account. Cash in the bank is the easiest thing for a plaintiff to go after. And remember, as our equity builds we would want to eventually isolate those properties into their own LLCs.

That said, I highly recommend using Series LLCs to manage multiple properties.

As we discussed earlier, Series LLCs allow us to set up a "parent" LLC and have multiple "series" tied to it. Each Series is treated as an independent LLC for asset-protection purposes. But its financial activity flows into the parent LLC's tax return.

So we get multiple LLCs under one roof with these. It's an incredible tool.

Now, we still need to set up a new bank account for each independent Series within the Series LLC. And we need to treat each Series as an independent entity. That's critical. But if we do this, we get top-tier asset protection without as much clutter.

That said, Series LLCs are only recognized by certain states. As I write, the states with advantageous laws around Series LLCs are: Alabama, Delaware, Iowa, Kansas, Nevada, Oklahoma, Tennessee, Texas, and Utah.

Keep in mind that this list is by no means a cosmic fixture. I would expect more states to jump on the Series LLC bandwagon over time. Series LLCs are relatively new. As such, I would recommend working with a professional to set them up.

There's one more step we have to cover. Our LLCs have to actually own the properties we are running through them if we want the asset protection.

I know that's obvious but remember, if we're doing conventional mortgages, the bank will require that we title the property in our personal name at closing.

We can still run that property through an LLC for tax and financial management purposes, but the LLC doesn't actually own the property if it's our name on the deed. Instead, we own it personally. That means if we are sued, that property is not protected.

The good news is that this is an easy fix. All we have to do is transfer the property's ownership to our LLC. The county courthouse can do this for us.

To do this, we must prepare a new warranty deed that conforms with the requirements within that particular state. That deed basically says that we are personally conveying ownership of the property to the LLC in exchange for consideration—maybe it's $10.

The deed must state that this transfer is subject to existing encumbrances on the property. That means we acknowledge the mortgage on the property is still valid and must be paid.

Once we have the new warranty deed prepared, we sign it in front of a notary and mail it to the county courthouse in the county where the property is located. Each county has a small recording fee that we'll have to pay... but that's it. Nothing more official than that needs to happen.

Once they record the new deed, our LLC will be the official owner of that property. Eventually the online systems will update to reflect this.

At this point we are about as buttoned up as we can be. If something happens on a property owned by an LLC, the plaintiff can't sue us personally. They can only sue the LLC. That means they only have access to the LLC's assets if they win.

If we're running our business correctly, the LLC's only assets are the cash it has in the bank and the equity it has in the property. This is why I build a six-month cash reserve for my LLCs and then distribute surplus funds to my personal account.

As for the LLC's equity, it's likely going to be small in the early days. But if we hold our properties for many years that equity will become substantial over time.

There's a nifty trick we can employ when we get to that point. We can create our own "funding company" and have it loan money to the LLC that's carrying significant equity. We would need to have a binding contract in place for this. But if we do it right, that loan becomes a claim on the LLC's equity. This is how we can use debt as an asset protection tool.

I would work with my asset-protection attorney to make sure everything was done by the book, but this can become a great tool for us as our rental portfolios grow.

To sum it all up—if we are diligent about asset protection, even if something bad happens with one property, it can't impact our other properties or any of our other assets. And that means we can't get wiped out by a stroke of bad luck. It's all about resiliency.

All right, before we close out I want to address a common concern around conventional mortgages.

If we were to actually read every little clause within the mortgage contract, somewhere in there it says that the lender has the right to call the note due in full if we transfer ownership of the property without their consent. Some point to this and say that we can't transfer conventionally financed properties into LLCs.

I don't see this as something to worry about. I've never had an issue with it, nor has anyone else in my investment network. The one thing that I was advised to do is to make sure that the LLC's ownership structure matches up with the note. Meaning, if the mortgage is in my name, I should be a primary member of the LLC as well.

The idea here is that if the lender were to notice that the property was in an LLC's name, the first thing they would do is check on who owned the LLC. If they see that it's the same person who financed the property—and then they see that all the payments come in on time—they have very little incentive to fuss about it.

And that's the key.

It's not in the lender's interest to call the note due in full. If the lender did take exception to the property being in an LLC, we could simply transfer ownership back to ourselves personally. It's the exact same process—not a big deal.

That said, this isn't going to be a foreign concept to any reputable lender. As long as we make all the payments on time, we shouldn't have any issues with deeding our properties into an LLC.

That concludes our chapter on asset protection. In Chapter Fourteen we'll talk about ways to accelerate our passive income.

Key Points

- Asset protection is about protecting our assets from lawsuits
- Asset protection has nothing to do with operations, taxes, or finances
- Good asset-protection strategies make it much more difficult for someone to sue us in the first place
- We should not associate all our accounts with our home address, personal cell phone number, and personal email address
- Umbrella insurance is a no-brainer
- When it comes to our properties, we should treat each property or groups of properties as their own independent business
- We should keep our properties and our LLCs isolated from one another—never commingle funds
- Series LLCs make asset protection easier to manage
- If we finance real estate in our name, we should transfer ownership into an LLC
- We can use debt from personal funding companies to enhance our asset protection

Action to take: I mentioned three services that can help make our online footprint less transparent to any attorney who is considering suing us.

Traveling Mailbox allows us to associate different mailing addresses with different accounts. MySudo allows us to use different phone numbers with our accounts. And ProtonMail allows us to use different email addresses.

You can get more information on these services on our resource page at: https://beyondthenestegg.com/extras/

CHAPTER FOURTEEN

ACCELERATING OUR PASSIVE INCOME

At this point in the book we now know how to use rental real estate to build passive income and reduce our tax bill substantially. The goal is financial independence.

If we can build a rental portfolio that generates $10,000 a month or more in passive income, and if we can eliminate our tax bill on that income, then most of us would be in a position where we didn't need to work a job anymore. We can spend our time doing only those things that are meaningful to us.

This is why I think rental real estate should be the cornerstone of our wealth strategy.

If we look at the total return, most of the time a rental portfolio will do better than a stock portfolio. More importantly, the returns we generate with our rental portfolio come in the form of cold hard cash that we can access at any time, for any reason.

As I shared earlier, my first goal with each rental property is to build up a cash reserve of at least $10,000 in the LLC's bank account. That's to cover repairs and emergencies. Once I've got my reserves in place, I typically distribute additional cash flow out to myself personally. This is money that I can use for anything I want.

Compare this to qualified retirement accounts like 401(k)s and IRAs where we are automatically hit with a 10 percent penalty if we take money out of those accounts before we reach the age 59 and a half. And then we have to pay taxes on the money we withdraw to boot. We get hit with taxes and a penalty for accessing our money.

To my way of thinking, that means the money in those accounts isn't really ours. At least not entirely. We can't even access it without paying the government for that privilege. This is just another way in which a wealth strategy based on real estate is superior to the traditional financial planning approach.

But there is a downside.

Building a rental portfolio is a rather slow and, oftentimes, a boring process at first. We have to save up enough money to put 20 percent down on each new property we buy, and that takes time, especially when we're dealing with larger new construction properties.

Coming up with our down payments becomes easier over time as we build equity in our first properties. We can tap into that equity to turn one property into two or three with no extra money out of pocket.

Of course, that's a few years down the road. It takes a while to get there. And sometimes we feel like we should be doing something while we're saving up for our next down payment. It can be hard to sit still for that long.

This gets people into trouble in the stock market. The need to do something prompts people to buy and sell stocks too frequently. I can say from my experience both as an investor and as a financial analyst that this is typically a mistake. To make money in the stock market, we need to buy great companies only when the price is right, and then we hold those companies for years.

So I want to share a few strategies with you that can speed up the process of building a rental portfolio. We'll start with perhaps the most traditional. Cash value life insurance.

I don't think that life insurance is very well understood today. For those who even think about it at all, Dave Ramsey's words are often what dominate their thoughts.

Ramsey famously advised people to "buy term and invest the difference."

That is, Ramsey suggested that people first compare the cost of cash value whole life insurance with term insurance. Then he suggested that they buy term insurance and invest the money they would have spent on cash value life insurance in mutual funds.

Keep in mind, term insurance is temporary coverage. If we don't die within the specified term, the policy expires and we aren't covered any more.

Whole life insurance is permanent. As long as we pay the annual premiums, the policy remains in place until we die.

These policies are more expensive than term policies… but there is a bonus. Whole life insurance policies pay dividends that build cash value. Cash value is money that we can use for anything we want, tax free.

No offense to Dave Ramsey, but his advice is very short-sighted.

Term life insurance will always be an expense for us—it does not generate a return or build cash value. Meanwhile, whole life insurance is an asset on our balance sheet. It pays us a dividend and builds cash value that we can tap into.

Dave Ramsey says to buy term and invest the difference. I say buy cash value whole life insurance and then invest the profits.

Life insurance is a powerful vehicle for warehousing tax-free wealth. Especially when you set up the policy to accelerate your cash value growth. This is something that only agents with specialized knowledge know how to do.

What does this have to do with real estate?

For those like me who are married with children, life insurance is a good idea. In my household, I'm the prominent income earner. I also manage all our finances. If something were to happen to me, my family would be in a tough spot.

As such, it's prudent for me to carry life insurance. If I were to die, my life insurance policies would send my family a large chunk of money, tax-free. Those funds would help them pick up the pieces and figure out how to go about things without me around.

As for my wife, she is the prominent childcare and education coordinator in the household. That's to say, she handles the kids' education and daily life experiences while I spend the days working. If something were to happen to her, I would be in a tough spot.

Therefore, it's prudent for her to carry life insurance. If she were to die, I would receive a lump-sum payment, tax-free. This would buy me time to figure out how to handle everything.

Now, we could do term policies to accomplish this. And as Dave Ramsey suggests, doing so would be much cheaper than buying cash value whole life insurance… in the short run.

However, strategically structured whole life policies will generate a return on investment every year. The return is very conservative—it's not going to impress us. But it's a return nonetheless. Properly structured whole life policies can be very profitable over time.

In this way, cash value life insurance policies are an asset for us. They produce a rate of return, tax-free—even though that's not the reason why we buy these policies. We buy them to support our families if something were to happen to us. Meanwhile, term life insurance policies will always be an expense on our balance sheet.

This is where strategy comes into play. We can borrow against our life insurance cash value at any time, for any reason. And again, that's not a taxable event. We don't owe taxes on money we borrow.

And guess what? There's no repayment schedule for cash value loans. We will have to pay a little bit of interest every year, but that's it. We can pay the loan back as fast or as slow as we want... or never at all.

I absolutely take advantage of this. I borrow against our life insurance cash value to help finance my real estate down payments. This helps me buy new properties sooner than I would otherwise be able to.

And that's where the next piece of this strategy comes into play.

I have two children. We don't need to carry life insurance on them, but buying insurance policies for children is dirt cheap.

What's more, it's not expensive to set up a policy for an infant that will grow its cash value to $80,000 or more by the time the child is in his or her twenties. That's a nice little chunk of change to get young people started in life.

This being the case, it is prudent for us to carry life insurance on our kids as well. Their policies are great savings mechanisms. Our goal is to transfer ownership of these policies to each child once they demonstrate that they are mature enough to handle the cash value responsibly.

But guess what? That's in the future. So until then, I borrow against their policies to buy more real estate.

For anyone with young children, cash value life insurance is a great idea. It's a savings vehicle for the kids. And it can help us build our rental portfolio until the kids are of age to take over their policies.

Again, the key is that we have to customize these policies correctly. Fortunately, it's not that hard to find an agent familiar with this approach. You just have to know what it is you're looking for. This is something we talk about quite a bit in our investment membership *The Phoenician League.*

Let's move on to a second trick. It pertains to crowdlending.

We talked about this earlier in the book, but crowdlending is an alternative to traditional bank financing. It allows investors to become the bank and lend money to borrowers for a specific purpose. Debt consolidation, home improvement, and medical expenses are three of the most common purposes.

This is done through a crowdlending platform.

Borrowers apply for the loan and provide their financial information. Then the platform pulls their credit report and assigns the loan a specific risk rating. This is what determines the interest rate.

From there the loan is added to the platform's investor portal. This allows investors to browse the listings and choose which loans they want to contribute to. In return, they receive monthly principal and interest payments, just like a bank.

What I love about this approach is that if we're consistently growing our loan portfolio, our passive income snowballs in a big way. Let's illustrate this with a few examples.

Suppose we start with $500 and begin building our crowdlending portfolio. Let's say we also kick in an extra $100 every week.

If we assume a 9.2 percent return on the portfolio, which is what I've experienced, we'll have a nest egg of $25,923 in four years' time.

Now let's say we start with the same $500, and then we kick in $200 more every week. Assuming the same rate of return, our portfolio will balloon to $51,182 in four years.

Who wouldn't want to turn $500 into $50,000 in just four years?

Here's the big thing—there's no market risk involved here. Unlike a stock portfolio, our loan portfolio will not fluctuate in value every day based on how the stock market moves.

That makes it possible to earn a high rate of return consistently.

Yes, some loans won't work out for us. But we account for that with equal position-sizing. Which is to say, we put the same amount of money into every loan we fund. If we're kicking in $100 or $200 a week, $25 per loan will do the trick.

This is a simple yet powerful way to build a small nest egg. The key is to take consistent action.

As I mentioned earlier, I was very skeptical about this kind of thing at first. I figured that the borrowers would consistently skirt their obligations and not make their payments. But to my surprise, almost all the borrowers pay on time. And it's not uncommon for borrowers to pay their loans off early.

For those working to save up money for real estate down payments, earning out-sized returns through crowdlending may be a good way to go.

I contribute $100 to my crowdlending portfolio every week. I use those funds to buy new notes according to my own risk assessment criteria. I also reinvest my interest income into new notes every month. This allows my portfolio to snowball very quickly.

My ultimate goal is to take these funds and use them to buy new rental properties. Crowdlending just helps me work up to my next 20 percent down payment faster.

The last thing we need to talk about is Bitcoin.

I trust that most everybody knows what Bitcoin is by now. However, I suspect many people still think that Bitcoin is little more than a speculative vehicle for millennials and aggressive traders.

In practice, Bitcoin is the hardest money the world has ever seen. That means bitcoins are incredibly scarce and no government, corporation, entity, or individual can create more of them on demand.

In this way Bitcoin is the exact opposite of the national fiat currencies that the world has used for the last five decades or so. That makes Bitcoin the perfect collateral for trade and high finance.

For real estate investors, there are several platforms out there now that will lend dollars against Bitcoin. I've used both BlockFi and Salt multiple times.

Unfortunately, BlockFi loaned a large sum of money to the digital asset exchange FTX, which turned out to be a fraud. When FTX collapsed, it took BlockFi down with it.

This speaks to the risks involved in borrowing dollars against Bitcoin. It should be remembered, however, that BlockFi was an early pioneer. This industry is only going to get bigger over time.

The idea is that anyone who owns a material position in Bitcoin can tap into its value without selling the underlying asset. We do this by borrowing dollars against our Bitcoin—and we then use those funds to finance real estate down payments.

Of course, this only makes sense if the monthly cash flow from our real estate acquisitions can cover both the new mortgage and our Bitcoin loan.

This also speaks to something the world's wealthiest families have known for a long time: At the end of the day, the name of the game is *debt and taxes.*

This runs counter to the conventional financial wisdom perpetuated by mainstream finance, but it's still a powerful concept.

All throughout history governments have sought to control the monetary system. They use their control to create new currency units out of thin air in order to support their pet programs. This effectively inflates away the value of the currency. That's why the purchasing power of the dollar and other fiat currencies has plummeted over the last one hundred years.

But look at the other side of the coin here.

As the purchasing power of the currency goes down, so does the real value of debt denominated in that currency. Here's what I mean…

If I owe $100,000 in debt and the purchasing power of the dollar falls by 10 percent over the next two years, in purchasing power terms that reduces my debt burden by the same 10 percent. Sure, the number still says $100,000… but $100,000 isn't what it used to be. Now it can buy 10 percent less than what it could before.

I know it's counterintuitive, but I'll explain this concept more. And let's start by extrapolating this out over decades…

The US dollar has lost over 87 percent of its purchasing power since 1970. That means $13,000 in 1970 could buy what $100,000 buys today. That's incredible to think about.

We see this in the fact that everything has gone up in nominal price. Rent, home prices, car prices, food prices… everything costs more in dollar terms today than it did in 1970. Much of that is simply a factor of the dollar's loss of value.

Keep in mind the fact that it's not more expensive to produce homes, cars, and food today. In most cases production costs have come down dramatically. The rising prices that we have seen are mostly explained by the dollar's fall in purchasing power.

We can also see this dynamic at work if we look at average income levels over time.

It was incredibly rare for anyone to have an annual income of $100,000 or more in 1970. That was super high-earner status.

Today plenty of people earn "six figures" a year. It's not that uncommon. The problem is, those six figures don't go nearly as far as they used to. Nobody earning $100,000 a year today is likely to consider themselves rich.

And that's where the magic is. I'll explain by applying this to real estate.

In our earlier discussion on analyzing real estate, we looked at two rental properties. One cost $325,000 and the other cost $128,000.

Let's focus on the $325,000 property here. That's probably a lot of money to most of us today. It's just not that easy to buy things that cost $325,000—even when we can finance 80 percent of the purchase.

But what's this going to look like ten years from now as the purchasing power of the dollar continues to fall? I wouldn't be surprised if $325,000 doesn't sound like that much anymore.

If we take out a 30-year fixed rate loan to buy that $325,000 house, our principal-and interest (P&I) mortgage payment will never change. Yet, our nominal income is likely to rise materially as the dollar's purchasing power falls, just as nominal incomes have risen dramatically since 1970.

That doesn't necessarily mean we will be making more money in real terms. We just established that somebody making $13,000 a year in 1970 had the same purchasing power as somebody making $100,000 today. Just because the number gets bigger, it doesn't mean we can actually afford to buy more stuff. That's because the price for stuff goes up too.

However, by fixing our mortgage payment, we put this dynamic to work in our favor.

As inflation eats away at the purchasing power of the dollar, our nominal income goes up as well. This is true of active income and it's true of rental income. As that happens, a fixed mortgage payment becomes much easier to pay, because it doesn't go up like everything else.

That's what I mean when I say that debt burdens fall as the value of the currency falls. The debt becomes easier to pay over time.

The big takeaway here is that debt is a powerful financial strategy, as long as we use it to acquire assets. I know it's common middle class advice to say "get out of debt." And that's true when we are talking about consumer debt.

When it comes to asset-backed debt at a fixed rate, it's not a bad move to get into debt. As crazy as that sounds, asset-backed debt is good within an inflationary monetary system like the one we have today. Debt puts the power of inflation to work for us.

Plus, debt is tax-advantaged. Let's get back to Bitcoin to illustrate this concept more.

I have borrowed against the same bitcoins several times to fund real estate down payments. Those loans are tax-free events. The dollars I receive from my Bitcoin loans are the dollars I get to spend. I don't have to pay taxes on them.

That wouldn't have been the case had I sold the bitcoins to fund my down payments. Had I sold, I would be on the hook for at least 15 percent in capital gains taxes, and potentially even more depending upon my income and how long I'd held the bitcoins.

What's more, I would have only been able to access the value of those bitcoins one time had I sold. I'd get the proceeds, and that's it. Then the bitcoins would be gone, and I would lose any future upside.

The same thing applies to real estate. Simply refinancing a property and taking out equity is a tax-free event. So you get tax-free dollars, and you still keep the asset.

Besides, all we are really doing with a cash-out refinance is pulling some or all of our down payment back out of the property. This allows us to use those same dollars to buy another property. Just like I've done with Bitcoin loans.

You see how this works?

Borrowing against assets we already own allows us to put the same dollars to work over and over again. And if we use these dollars to buy more assets, this process grows exponentially over time.

What about if we want to sell a piece of real estate? In most cases, that's going to be a more efficient way to tap into our gains.

We can use either a 1031 exchange or accumulated carry-over losses to mitigate our taxes when we sell a property. We talked about how carry-over losses work earlier in the book.

As for 1031 exchanges, this is a process that allows us to roll the gains from a real estate sale into new real estate purchases tax free—as long as we follow all the rules. This allows us to defer paying taxes on our real estate gains indefinitely.

I'd wager that most of us have friends and acquaintances who we know make a lot of money at their jobs. Yet, many of these good people don't seem to get ahead as much as one would think given their income level. Some even seem to struggle.

This has a lot to do with the old adage—it's not what you make, it's what you keep.

My heart goes out to those people. They are probably operating on bad rules and bad advice. Much of this bad advice is probably well intentioned. But some of it isn't. We have to be careful who we listen to.

But you know, life just doesn't need to be that hard. To get ahead, all we have to do is play the game. It's called *debt and taxes.*

The rules of the game are very simple. Acquire cash-flowing assets with fixed debt. Follow the tax code to reduce or eliminate taxes. Buy more cash-flowing assets.

Do this and financial independence is all but baked into the cake. We can grow our passive income such that it covers all of our expenses. At that point we can spend our time doing only things that are important and truly meaningful to us.

That brings me to a final point I want to make. I truly think there needs to be a higher purpose to all of this.

I have worked with more than a few incredibly intelligent, ambitious, and successful people in my career. Over time, I noticed that the calmest of these people didn't seem to care much about money or net worth. They seemed focused on a higher purpose.

The more I became receptive to the thought of having a higher purpose, the more a clear vision of my own higher purpose started to form in my mind. Almost like magic. There's something incredibly powerful about our subconscious mind.

The vision that formed in my head is one reason why I was motivated to write this book. I think all human beings should be financially independent, and I think it's easier to get there than ever before today. There's just way more noise clouding our judgment today than there used to be.

If you would like additional support as you walk your path, please check out *The Phoenician League.* Our investment membership was designed specifically to help people work up to $10,000 a month in passive income—far faster than most believe possible.

Key Points

- If we can build a rental portfolio that generates $10,000 a month or more in passive income, and if we can eliminate our tax bill on that income, then most of us would be in a position where we didn't need to work a job anymore
- This is why rental real estate should be a cornerstone of our wealth strategy
- Building a rental portfolio is a slow process at first

- A special approach to cash value life insurance can accelerate our ability to buy real estate
- Building a crowd-lending portfolio can help us buy an extra property every three to five years
- Leveraging Bitcoin is another way to accelerate our real estate acquisitions
- Asset-based debt is a great hedge against inflation
- We can use 1031 Exchanges to sell our real estate and avoid paying capital gains taxes
- Having a higher purpose is important

Action to take: If you're interested in learning more about our investment membership *The Phoenician League,* you can find more information on our program and our vision right here: https://phoenicianleague.com/secret/

CHAPTER FIFTEEN

A CASE STUDY FOR BUILDING $10,000 A MONTH

At this point you have all the knowledge you need to build financial security and start working toward financial independence. Now it's just a matter of putting that knowledge into practice.

As we've discussed, the traditional approach to retirement just isn't in our best interests. There are too many restrictions. Too many uncertainties. And too much left to chance.

In fact, the traditional model forces us to take the roundabout way to retirement. It herds us into piecemeal investments that we buy today, hoping only to sell them years down the road.

This approach puts us on a see-saw. In our working years we pour our savings into financial assets, then when we retire we sell those assets to create income for ourselves. When our assets are going up, we don't have extra income. Then when we want more income, we have to sell our assets.

It's always a choice between assets and income. That's the see-saw.

The problem is, our financial situation becomes precarious as we sell off our assets. It gets to the point where we can't afford unplanned expenses. And then we have to spend our retirement worrying about money.

At *The Phoenician League*, we pursue a better way.

It starts with taking the current macroeconomic picture into full account. We assess the monetary system and the big-picture macro trends, then we create a customized asset allocation model accordingly. This model provides us with financial security.

From there we focus nearly 100 percent on creating passive income for ourselves. We do this with a turn-key approach to rental real estate. Real estate may not be flashy, but there's simply no better vehicle for truly passive income.

That's because real estate compounds our returns in multiple ways. And that's regardless of whether or not our properties go up in value.

What's more, real estate provides us with massive tax advantages. And make no mistake about it—we have a system in place that makes building passive income with real estate automatic.

With our training program and our infrastructure, acquiring cash-flowing rental properties is nearly as simple as buying stocks online. It's just a matter of browsing the online property portal and picking out the properties we like. The network handles the rest.

The end result is that we shouldn't have to spend more than ten minutes a week on our real estate portfolio most of the time. Our professional network puts everything on autopilot for us. Then the rent checks just show up in our bank accounts each month.

This is the fast track to $10,000 a month in passive income.

And think about what will happen when we have an extra $10,000 coming in every month like clockwork. For most of us, we should be financially independent at that point. We won't be dependent on a job or an active business. Which is to say, we won't need to work for money anymore. We can scrap the rat-race.

Then the whole idea of retirement goes out the window. It doesn't matter if we're 45 or 65—we're good. We can spend our time doing only things that are truly important to us.

That's the vision.

The Phoenician League is the solution. It's how we get there. Our goal is to help every single member achieve financial freedom.

We've got the system in place to make that possible. We've got the professional network on call to make it turn-key. And we've got a great community that ensures every member gets all the support they need to walk the journey.

To illustrate this, let's walk through a case study.

Mike's Path to $10,000 a Month in Passive Income

The Phoenician League isn't just another information product. We explicitly help members take the direct path to financial independence. It's all about the infrastructure and the network.

Take Mike W.'s story, for example. Mike got started down his path to financial freedom in 2019.

Mike started with the core training program. Then he bought his first rental property in November 2019. At the time it generated just over $800 a month in passive income.

Now, $800 a month is hardly life-changing. But it's a great starting point. And that's exactly how Mike treated it.

He let the cash flow from that first property build up six months' worth of reserve. Then he set his sights on acquiring his next property. That happened in June of 2020. The second rental also produced just over $800 a month in cash flow.

Again, Mike let that property's cash flow build up a six-month reserve fund, and then he went looking for his next acquisition.

Now that he had over $1,600 a month in extra income coming in, buying the third property was much easier. Mike added his third rental in March 2021. It produced about $660 a month in cash flow.

In just sixteen months Mike had worked up to over $2,260 a month in passive income. All leveraging *The Phoenician League's* resources.

Then he kept going.

Mike added his fourth property in August 2021. Then he picked up properties number five and number six in 2022. By the time the calendar flipped to 2023, Mike had $4,131 in rental income coming in every single month. That means he went from $0 to over $4,000 in just over three years.

Keep in mind this is 100 percent passive income. Mike's not managing these properties himself. He has professional property managers doing all the work for him.

And get this, by 2023 Mike's first property alone was kicking out $1,150 a month in cash flow. That's because market rents went up every single year after he bought in 2019.

How amazing is that?

This speaks to the fact that, if you follow our process, everything starts to snowball. Your passive income growth may seem a bit slow in the first few years, but it will gain steam over time.

Now think about this. Mike has his path to $10,000 a month in passive income already mapped out. He's on track to hit that target in early 2026. If he stays on course, Mike will have gone from $0 to $10,000 a month in just over six years. That's the power of our approach to financial independence.

Mike can accurately plan out his progress because he's plugged into a nationwide real estate network. He knows exactly what kind of properties are available at any given time, and he knows exactly what kind of cash flow he could get from these properties.

With those connections, it's just a matter of adding the right properties to his portfolio. And it becomes easier and easier to add new properties as he builds equity and generates tax advantages. Everything snowballs over time.

If you asked Mike, he would tell you that his first property was by far the hardest to buy. He was equipped with our core training and he was plugged into our network, but he had no proof the system would work.

Fast forward to today and Mike has over $4,000 of passive income coming at him, month in and month out. It's like clockwork.

Naturally, this makes it much easier for Mike to add new properties to his portfolio. Three more years and he should be at the $10,000-a-month mark.

As you can see, nothing about this is rocket science, nor does it require any luck. We don't have to hit it big on any one investment.

Instead, we take a systematic approach. It's not flashy, but it works.

Best of all, none of this is tedious or time consuming. With our resources and our network, working up to $10,000 a month should take no more than ten minutes a week. That's it.

And remember, with *The Phoenician League*, you'll have direct support every step of the way. Together, we'll make financial freedom a simple step-by-step process.

If you would like to explore our membership more, you can find us right here: https://phoenicianleague.com/secret/

Now, let's wrap up this book by talking about the picture. Let's talk about our 'why.'

CHAPTER SIXTEEN

BECOMING A GOOD STEWARD OF CIVILIZATION

Congratulations for making it to the very end of the book.

At this point you've absorbed all the information around finance and economics that we have to offer. I know it's a data dump. Much of it may take some time to sink in. But I trust that there are at least a few ideas in here that will bear fruit for you in the years to come.

That said, we have one more topic to discuss, and I think it's the most important of all. Let's talk about being a good steward of civilization.

Here's the thing. My observations suggest that most people simply don't have the drive or the willpower to become financially independent.

As we've discussed in this book, the process for achieving financial independence isn't overly complicated. Sure, the mechanics around LLC's and advanced tax strategies may appear to be convoluted at first, but they really aren't that difficult to manage once you know what you are doing.

I think for the most part everything else we've discussed is fairly simple and straightforward. These are steps that anybody can take. It's a path that anybody can walk.

But it does take work, vision, and commitment to make it all happen. For whatever reason, many people just don't want to do the work. They would rather collect their paycheck during the week and live for the weekend.

I don't want to knock that. It's a choice, and everybody should be free to make their own choices.

But I do think that those of us who have the drive to become financially independent also have the responsibility to do so. And that's because I don't think we can truly become a good steward of civilization otherwise. If we are stuck in the rat race, we just don't have the time, money, or energy we need to also work on projects that might benefit our communities.

This is why I'm so passionate about finance and investing. If we are financially independent, we will have the time and the resources to found and support civil service programs in our communities in a strictly voluntary way.

We can take the time to really explore what's going on in our community. We can assess what's happening in our city, our town, our county… and we can gauge what problems need to be solved. Then we can figure out how to solve them in ways that do not force anyone to pay for our programs against their will. Everything can be voluntary.

For example, I live in a rural place. There's only one major employer in the area. So there aren't very many traditional jobs available.

Yet, I look around and see a wealth of opportunity.

For starters, it's not easy to get contractors, electricians, HVAC specialists, or plumbers to come out for small jobs or routine repairs. That's because there just aren't that many of them in rural locations like this. And the ones that are here are already swamped.

What's more, the individuals who own these businesses are now in their sixties and seventies. They would love to sell their companies and retire, but they have nobody to sell to. The ambitious young people went off to college and never came back.

That's a tremendous opportunity. Anyone looking for work could do a paid internship and learn one of these trades directly from somebody who's been in it for decades. Then that person would have a high-paying career path in front of them.

And if they learned a little bit about business and finance in their spare time, that person could position themselves to buy the entire company in five or six years. It's right there for the taking.

That would enable them to earn even more money. And they would become a staple in the local community. The community would benefit tremendously as well. We need these service-oriented businesses to continue to function for generations to come.

Could we develop a program to help young people looking for work link up with opportunities to learn one of these trades that are in high demand? That's a worthy project for somebody who's not stuck in the rat race anymore.

The same program could also teach people how to become internet-based entrepreneurs. That would expand its reach even more. And it would benefit local communities tremendously as well.

Those of us who earn income online are basically mini-stimulus plans for the local community. We earn money from outside the area, then we spend it at businesses inside the community. That creates revenue for local businesses.

This is just one example of many. There are all kinds of problems and challenges that we can tackle once we don't have to spend all our time and energy working for money anymore.

Western civilization, and specifically the American experiment, was founded upon this idea that anyone can rise up to be a leader in the community. These principles were passed down from generation to generation to ensure that our civilization carried onward.

When I think about this kind of thing, I can't help but feel a direct link to the past.

Those of us in developed countries today are blessed to live in a world of abundance. Most of us probably take this for granted, but we shouldn't.

We owe those who came before us an immense debt of gratitude for the foundation they left us with. At the same time, I think we have a responsibility to leave our kids and grandkids with a strong foundation as well.

Part of our civilization's advancement came from our mindset. Each generation had the idea that it should advance farther than the one that came before—both with regards to education and financial well-being.

This idea was often referred to as "generational progress." And it was largely accepted by both parents and their children for several generations.

In recent years, this idea has started to fade. Many in our society no longer believe that generational progress is still possible. To me, this speaks to the failure of the "nest egg" approach to personal finance and the entire concept of "retirement."

If we build a robust asset allocation model as suggested in this book, then we are also building a timeless foundation that can last for generations.

Then if we can use that foundation as a jump-off point to build passive income with rental real estate, we'll have the makings of a family empire. If we do proper estate planning, the tax code allows us to pass our empire on tax-free to the next generation.

When we put the two together, then we can set our kids and our grandkids up to start on a higher platform than we did. Add in a few strategic life insurance policies as discussed in this book and the idea of generational progress could be immediately revived. It's all right there in front of us.

I would like to leave you with a quotation that I keep on my desk and read every day.

"Behold, I send you forth as sheep in the midst of wolves. Be ye therefore wise as serpents and harmless as doves."

This is from the Bible's book of Matthew. It's Chapter 10, Verse 16. But I don't think one needs to be Christian or even religious to see how it applies to us today.

My friends, we are the ones we've been waiting for. Like those who came before us, let us not neglect our duty to steward civilization another generation forward.

Instead, let's create. Let's collaborate. And let's build networks and structures that will last for generations.

We have a tremendous opportunity in front of us. Let's seize the day.

Thank you.

Key Points

- Most people simply don't have the drive or the willpower to become financially independent
- Achieving financial independence takes work, vision, and commitment
- Those of us who do have the drive to become financially independent also have the responsibility to do so
- Becoming financially independent enables us to become good stewards of civilization
- We are the ones that we've been waiting for

NOW IT'S YOUR TURN

Would you like help implementing what you've learned in this book? *The Phoenician League* will walk with you every step of the way. We provide the training, the investments, the professional connections, and the one-on-one support you need to hit your goals and achieve financial independence.

If you would like to learn more about our investment membership – what we do and how we do it – please see our information page right here:

https://phoenicianleague.com/secret/

Our goal is to help everyone build a customized asset allocation model and work up to having $10,000 a month in extra income. We have a 7-step process for making it all happen. And we have a great core group of members who will support you every step of the way.

See you inside.

ABOUT THE AUTHOR

Joe Withrow has nearly two decades' worth of experience in finance. He started his career in corporate banking. Then he became an investment analyst within the largest financial research network on the planet. Joe's an expert investor, the author of three books, and the founder of an investment membership called *The Phoenician League*. In his spare time, Joe enjoys reading, philosophy, kayaking, and spending time with his two children.

Can You Help?

Thank You For Reading My Book!

I really appreciate all of your feedback, and I love hearing what you have to say. Would you take the time to leave me an honest review on Amazon letting me know what you thought of the book?

Thanks so much. Here's to your financial independence!

—Joe Withrow

Made in United States
Orlando, FL
04 August 2024

49922440R00124